HOW TO DRAW CHIBI

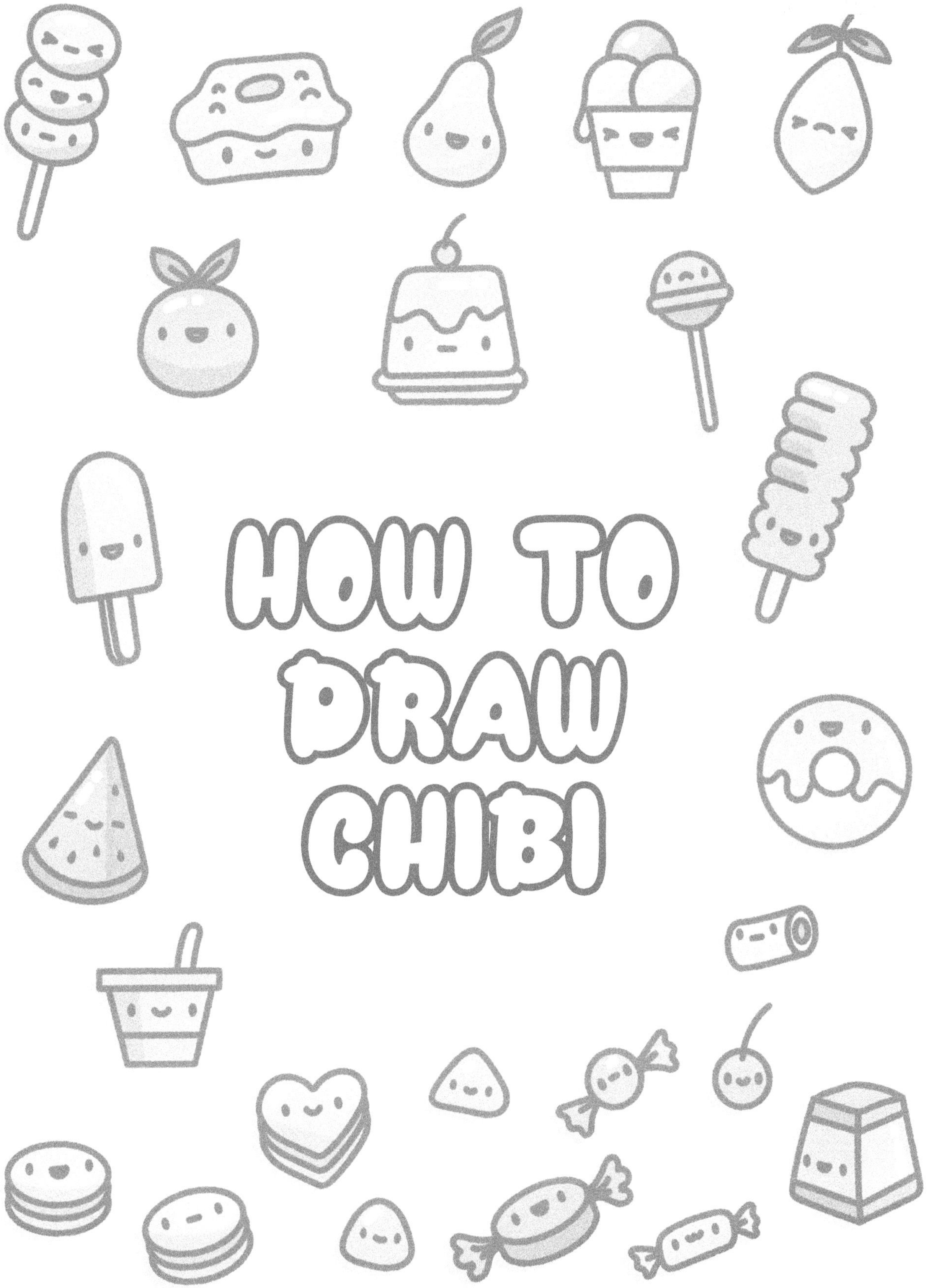

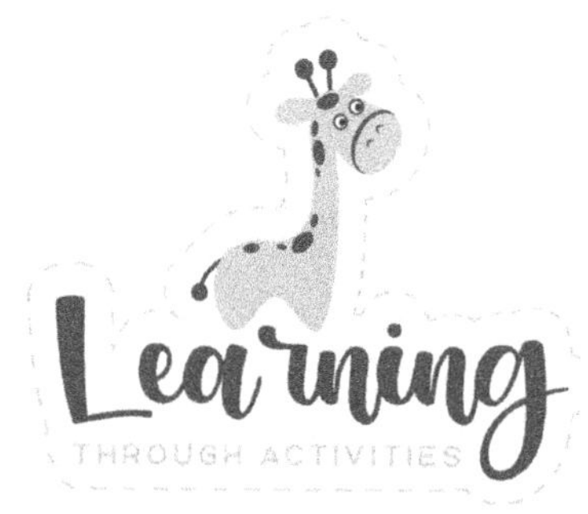
Learning
THROUGH ACTIVITIES

SPECIAL BONUS!

Want These 2 Books For FREE?

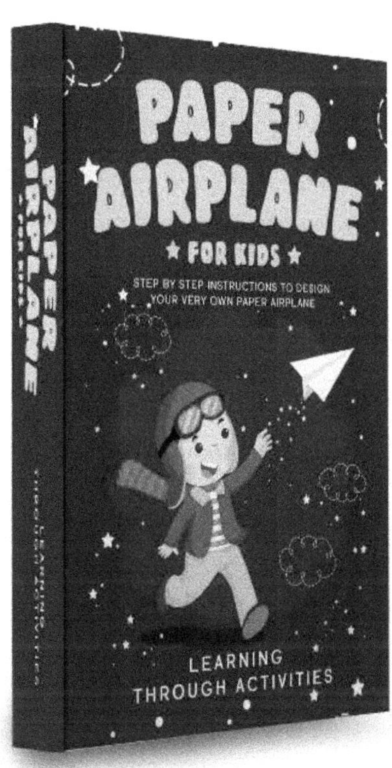

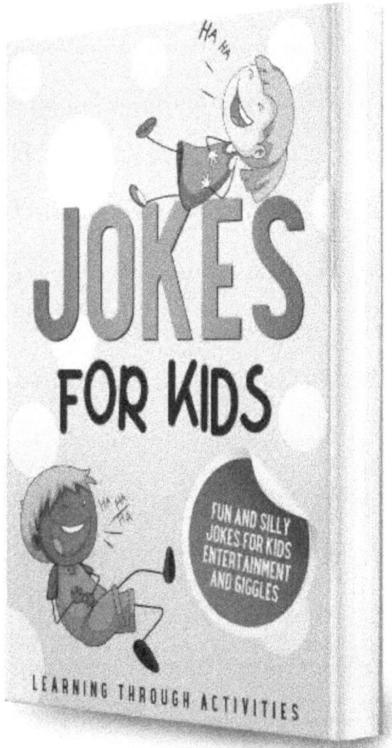

Get FREE, unlimited access to these and all of our new kids books by joining our community!

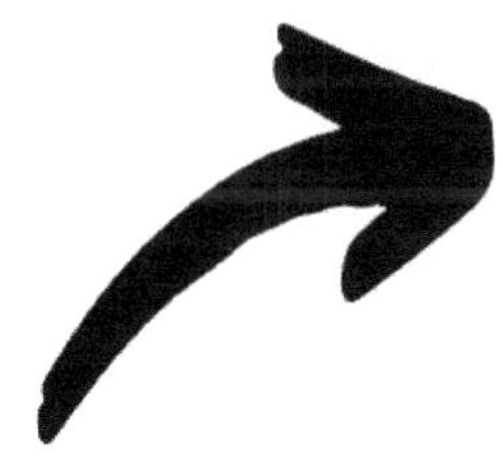

Scan W/ Your Camera To Join!

CONTENTS

INTRODUCTION

WELCOME TO 'HOW TO DRAW CHIBI.' THIS BOOK IS FULL OF ALL DIFFERENT KINDS OF FUN, CUTE CHARACTERS! YOU'LL BE AN ARTIST BEFORE YOU KNOW IT!

EACH CHIBI HAS EASY TO FOLLOW INSTRUCTIONS THAT WILL STEP-BY-STEP HAVE YOU DRAWING THEM LIKE A PRO!

NOT ONLY WILL YOU LEARN HOW TO DRAW ALL OF THESE CHIBI CHARACTERS, YOU WILL ALSO LEARN WHERE EACH OF THEM LIVE AND WHAT THEY LOVE!

PLEASE DON'T WORRY IF YOUR CHIBI CHARACTERS TURN OUT A LITTLE DIFFERENT FROM THE ONES IN THE PICTURES, WE ALL HAVE OUR UNIQUE STYLE, AND ALSO, PRACTICE MAKES PERFECT!

GENERALLY, IT'S BEST TO START WITH A PENCIL WHILE YOU ARE GETTING THE HANG OF IT, SO LITTLE MISTAKES CAN BE EASILY ERASED. THEN MOVE ONTO PENS, COLORED, SPARKLY, WHATEVER YOU LIKE.

HAVE FUN!

EYES

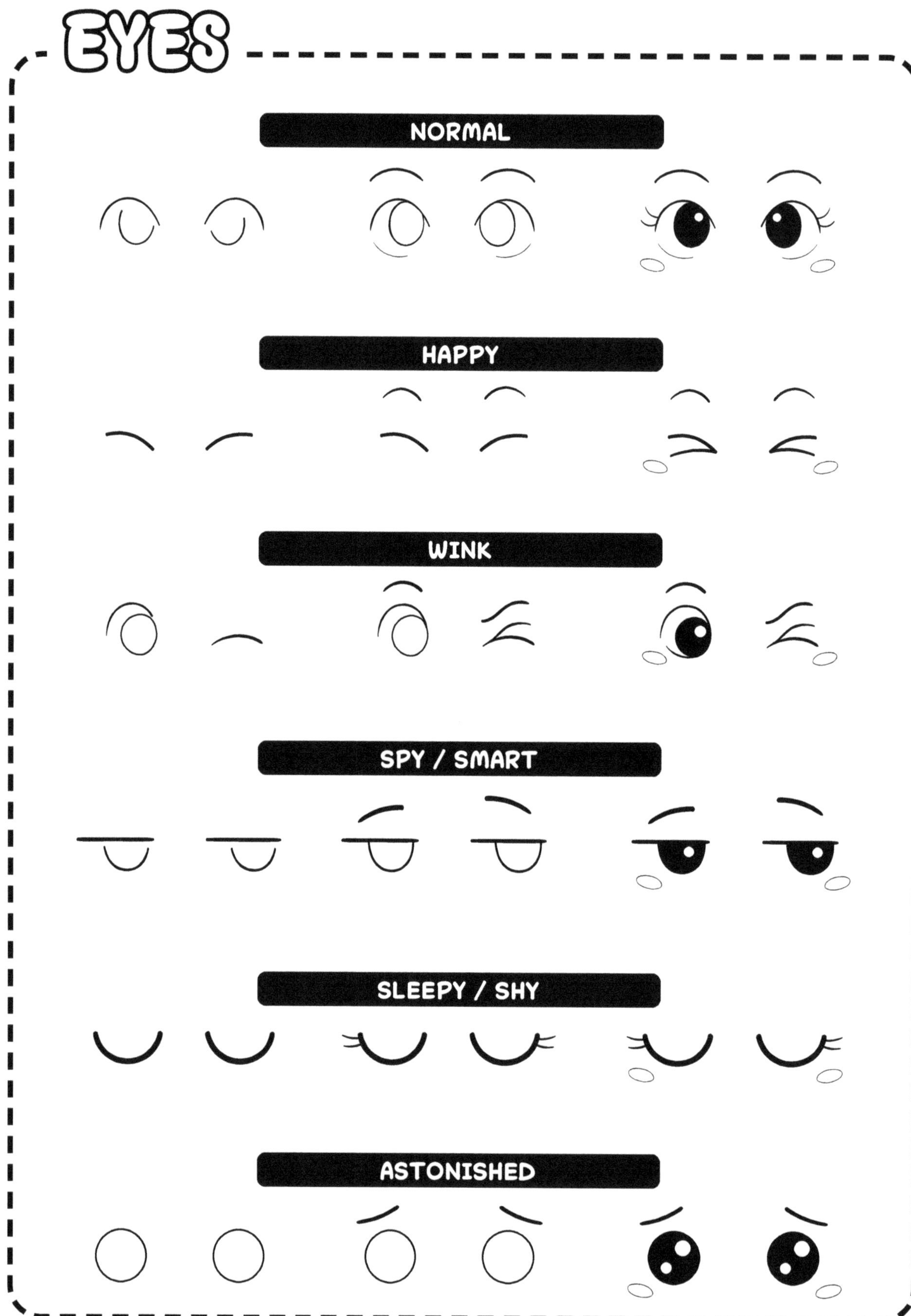

TUMBLY

LIVES:

IN AN ENGLISH ZOO, AND IS SO SPOILED.

LOVES:

PLAYING WITH ANTS, BUT IS AFRAID OF SQUISHING THEM!

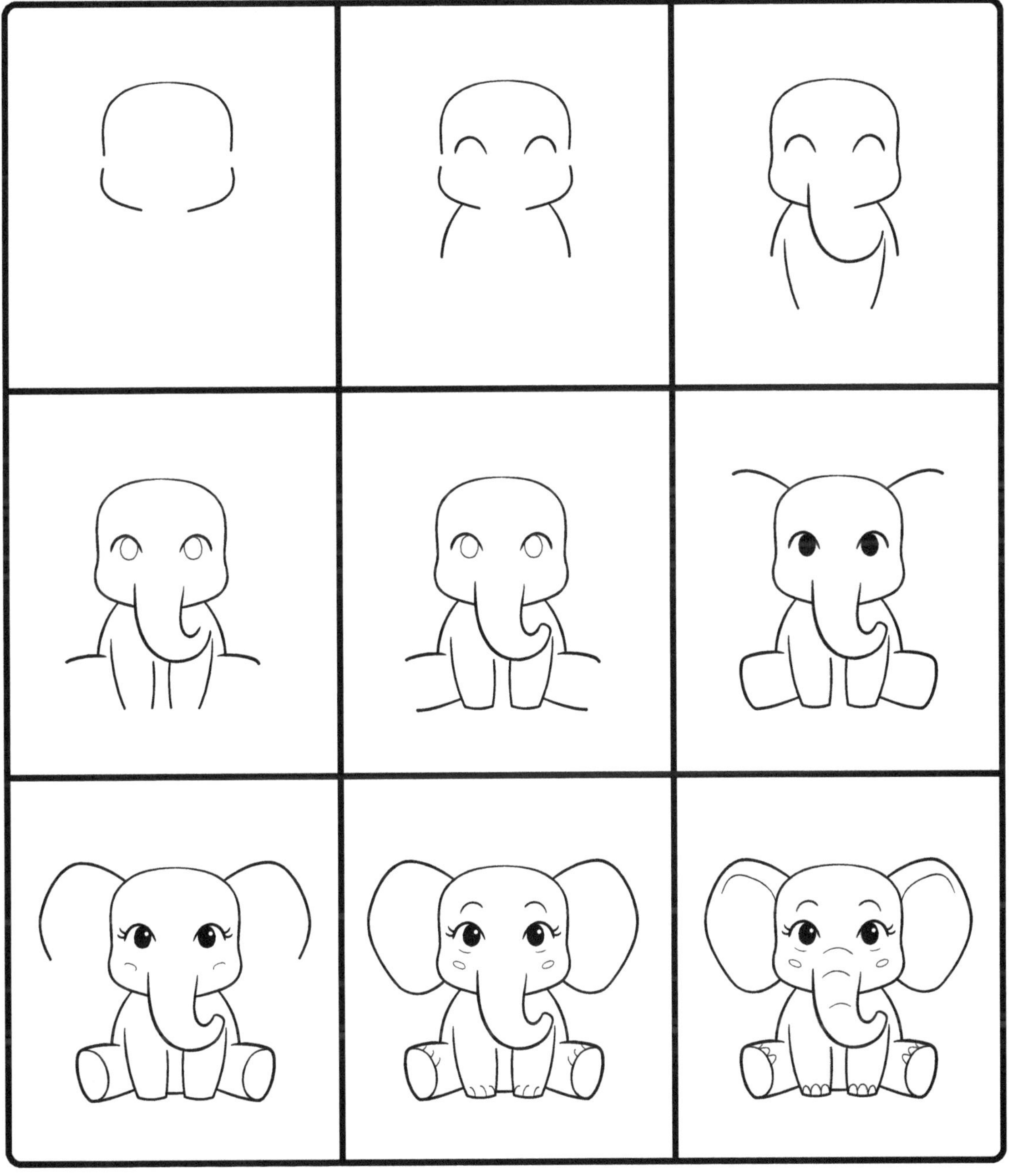

TEEBEE

LIVES:

IN A LITTLE GIRL'S BEDROOM IN A CABIN IN THE WOODS.

LOVES:

THE WOODS, BUT IS NOT A REAL BEAR AND SO IS ALWAYS STUCK INSIDE.

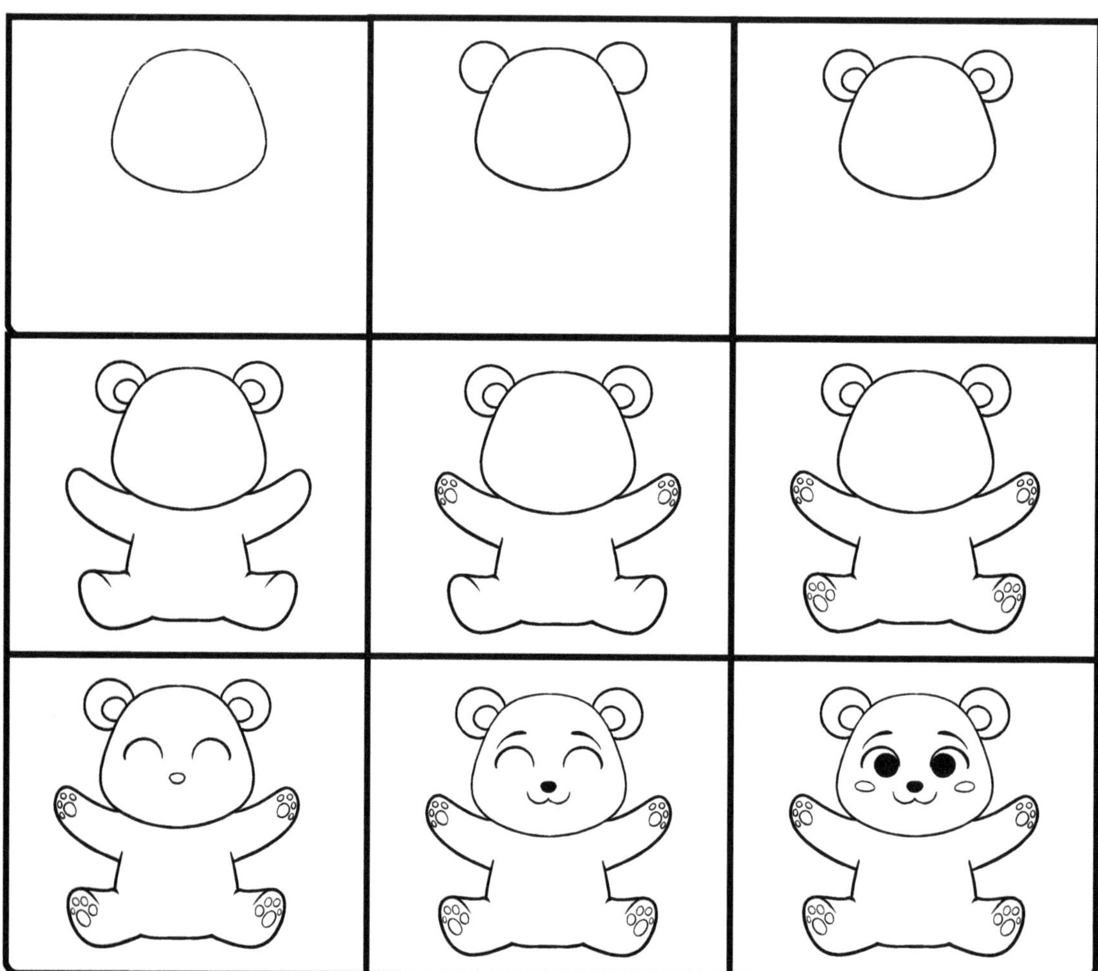

BOUNCE

LIVES:

WITH A YOUNG FAMILY AND THEIR SILLY CAT.

LOVES:

ROLLING IN THE DIRT AFTER A BATH, BUT HE ALWAYS GETS IN TROUBLE, WHY?

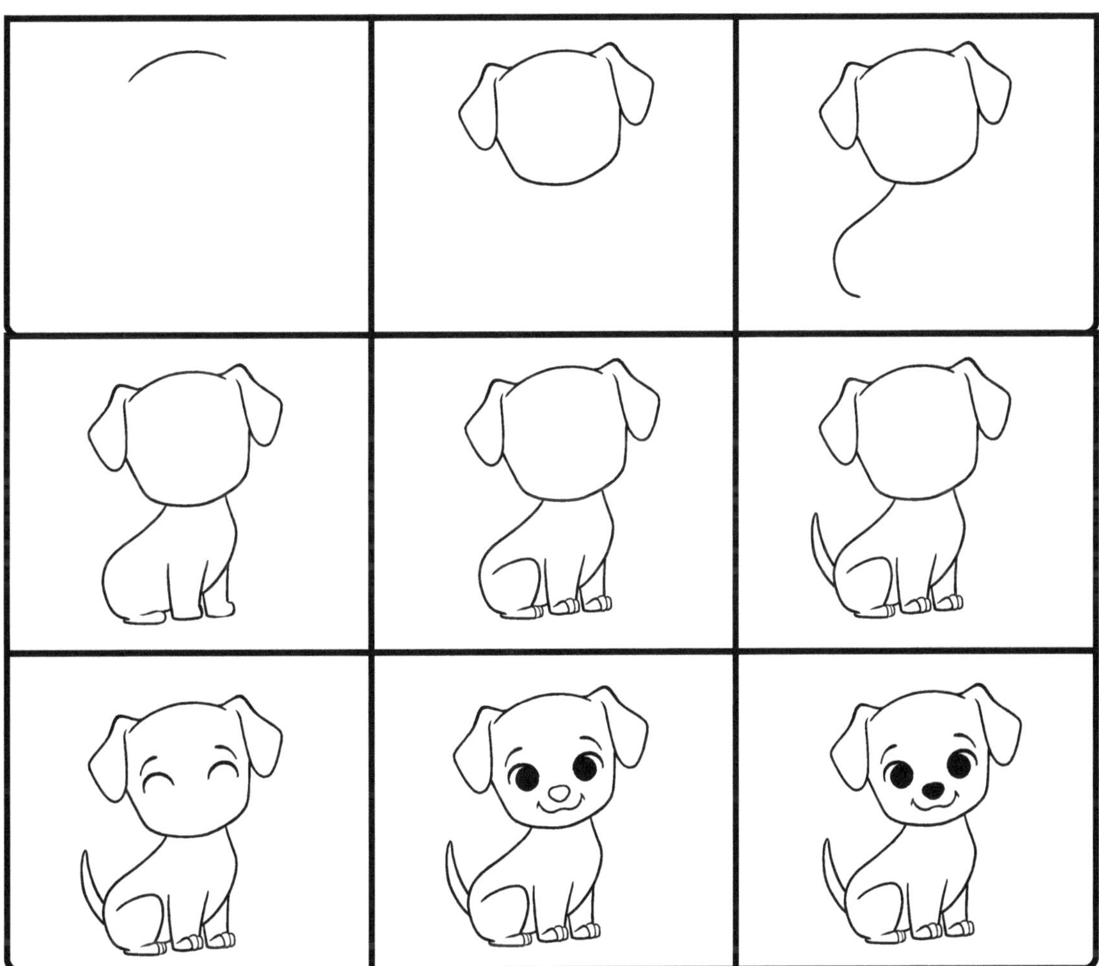

CONNIE

LIVES:

LIVES ON A BALCONY IN FRANCE.

LOVES:

A BOY CAT ACROSS THE ROAD, BUT SHE'S NEVER ALLOWED OUTSIDE.

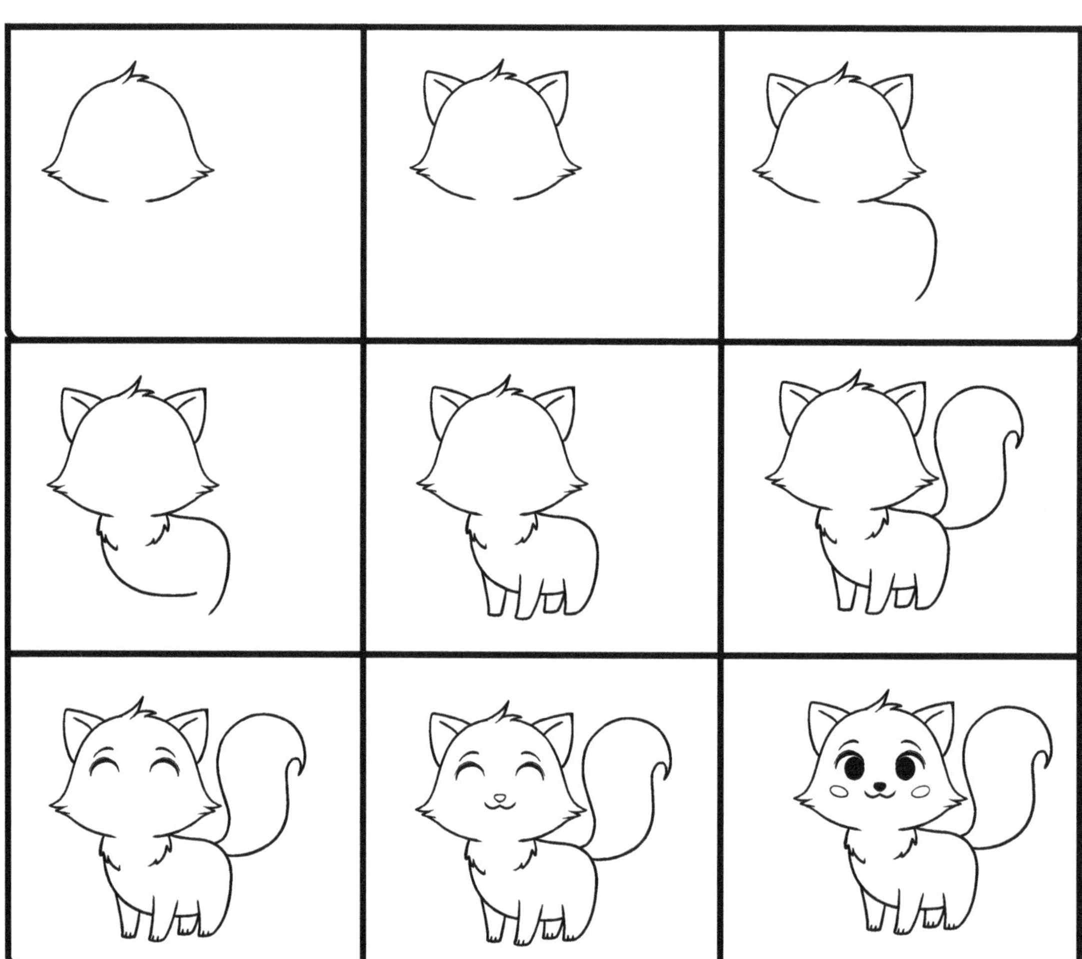

CURL-TOP

LIVES:

IN AN ICE CREAM SHOP BY THE BEACH.

LOVES:

GOING TO THE BEACH, BUT HE MELTS IN A MINUTE!

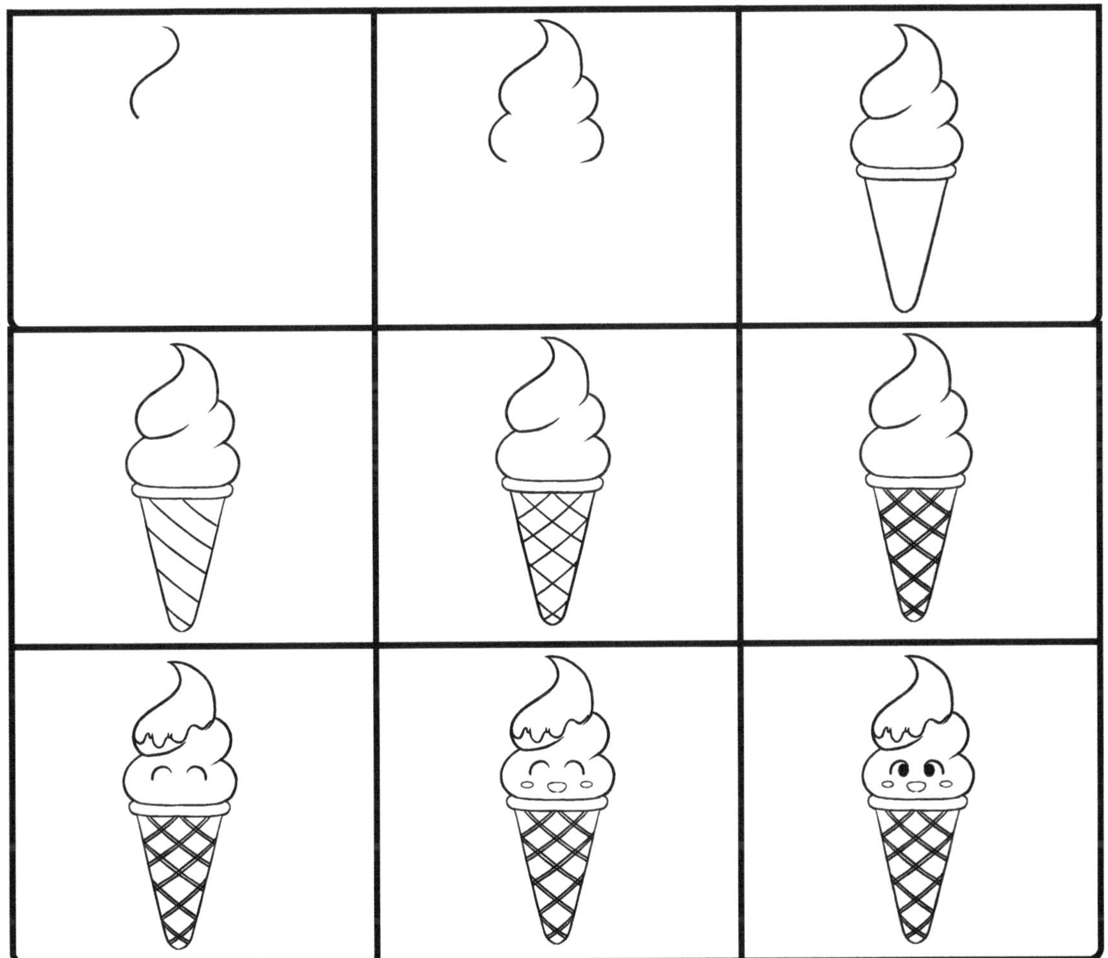

CEE-CEE

LIVES:

IN A POT IN A CHILD'S YARD.

LOVES:

BALLOONS, BUT THEY ALWAYS POP!

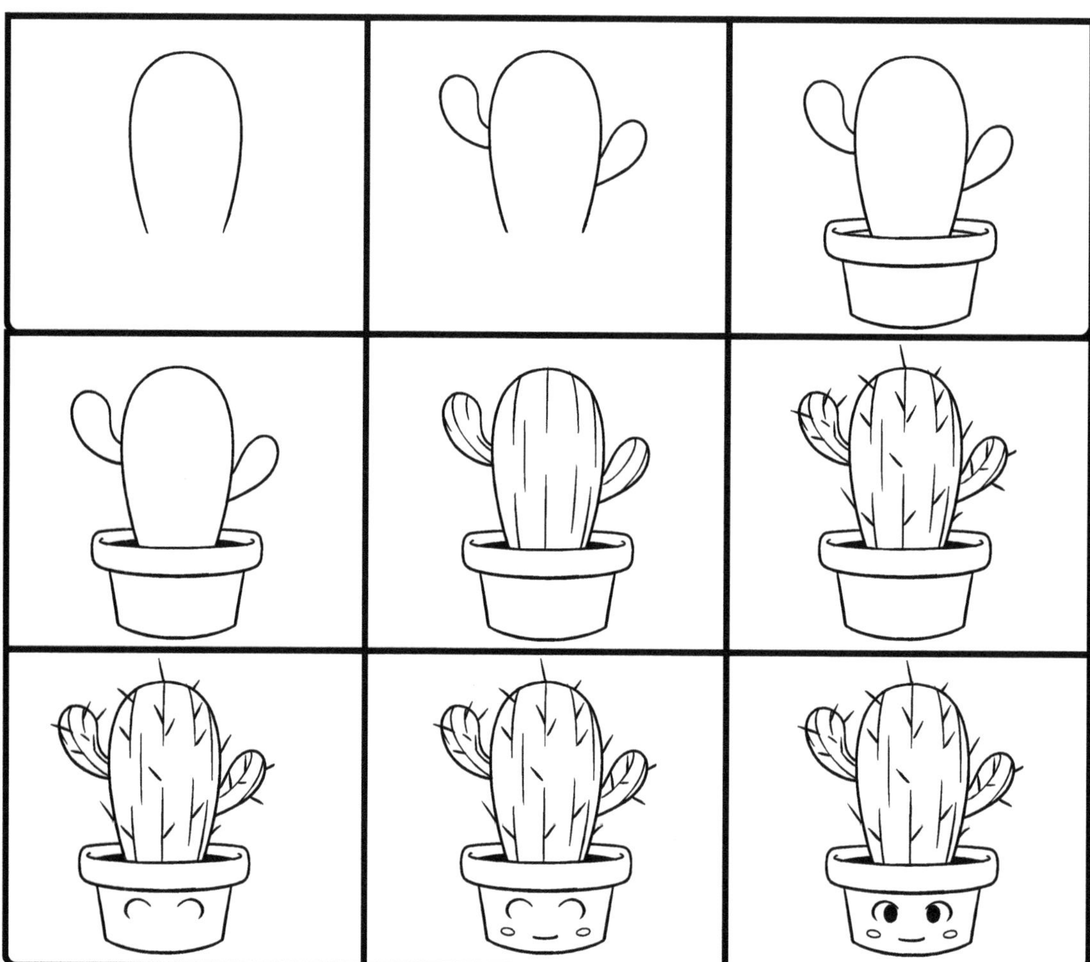

SUNSHINE

LIVES:

AT A JUICE BAR.

LOVES:

BEING MIXED UP WITH OTHER JUICES, BUT NEVER VEGGIES, UGH!

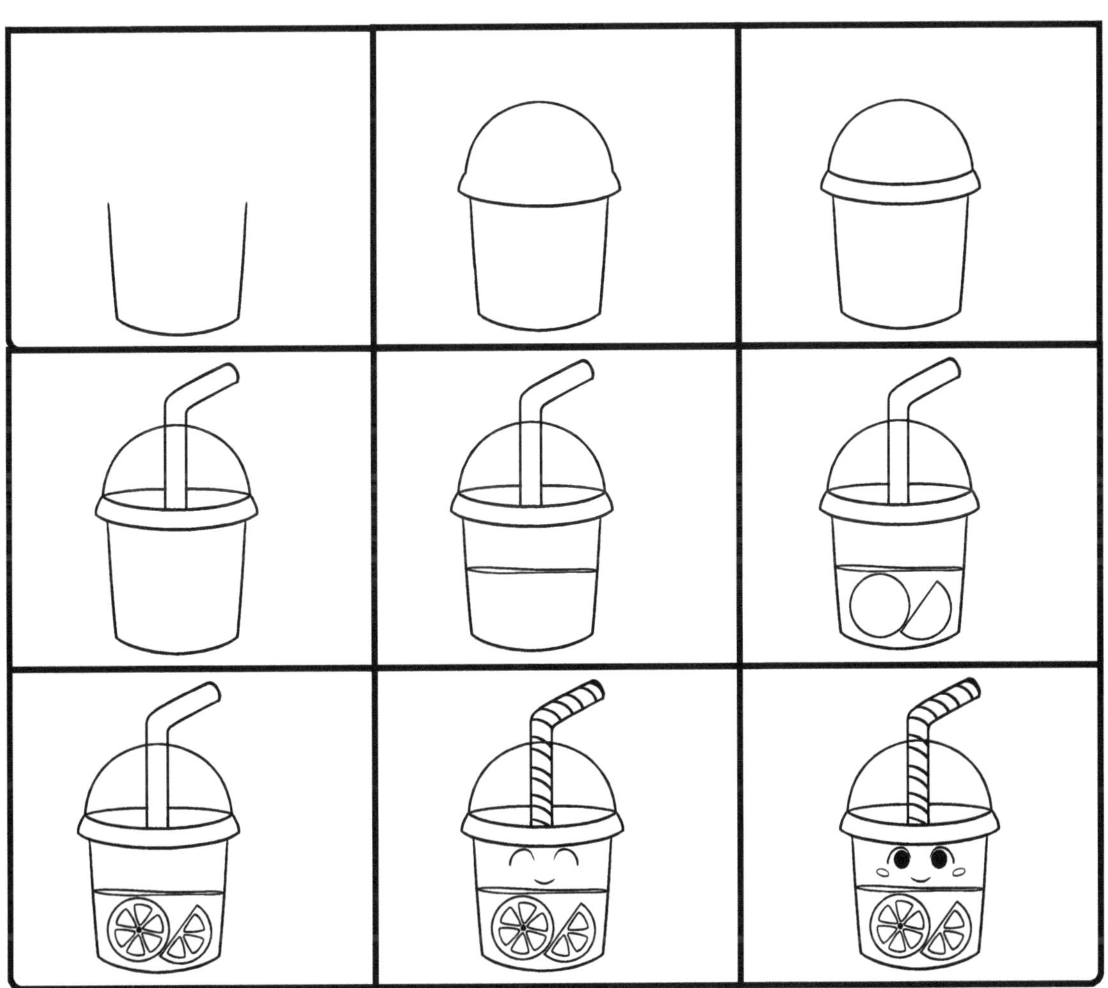

SWEETY

LIVES:

IN A WARREN NOT FAR FROM A LOVELY SANDY BEACH.

LOVES:

HOW SOFT HER FLUFFY TAIL IS, AND HOPPING AS HIGH AS SHE CAN.

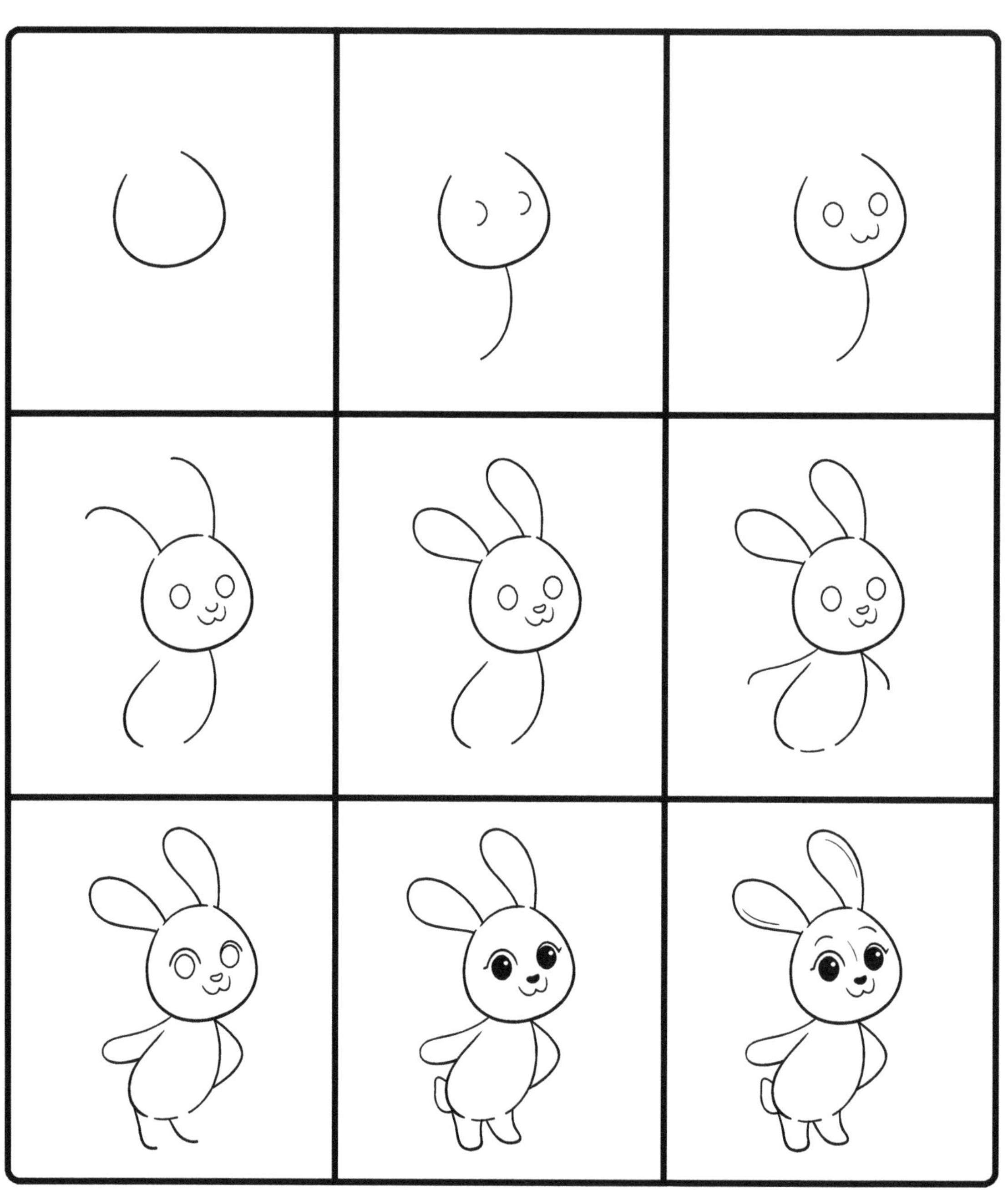

TIGS

LIVES:

IN LONG TALL GRASS.

LOVES:

PLAYING HIDE AND SEEK, BUT NO ONE EVER FINDS HIM, EVER.

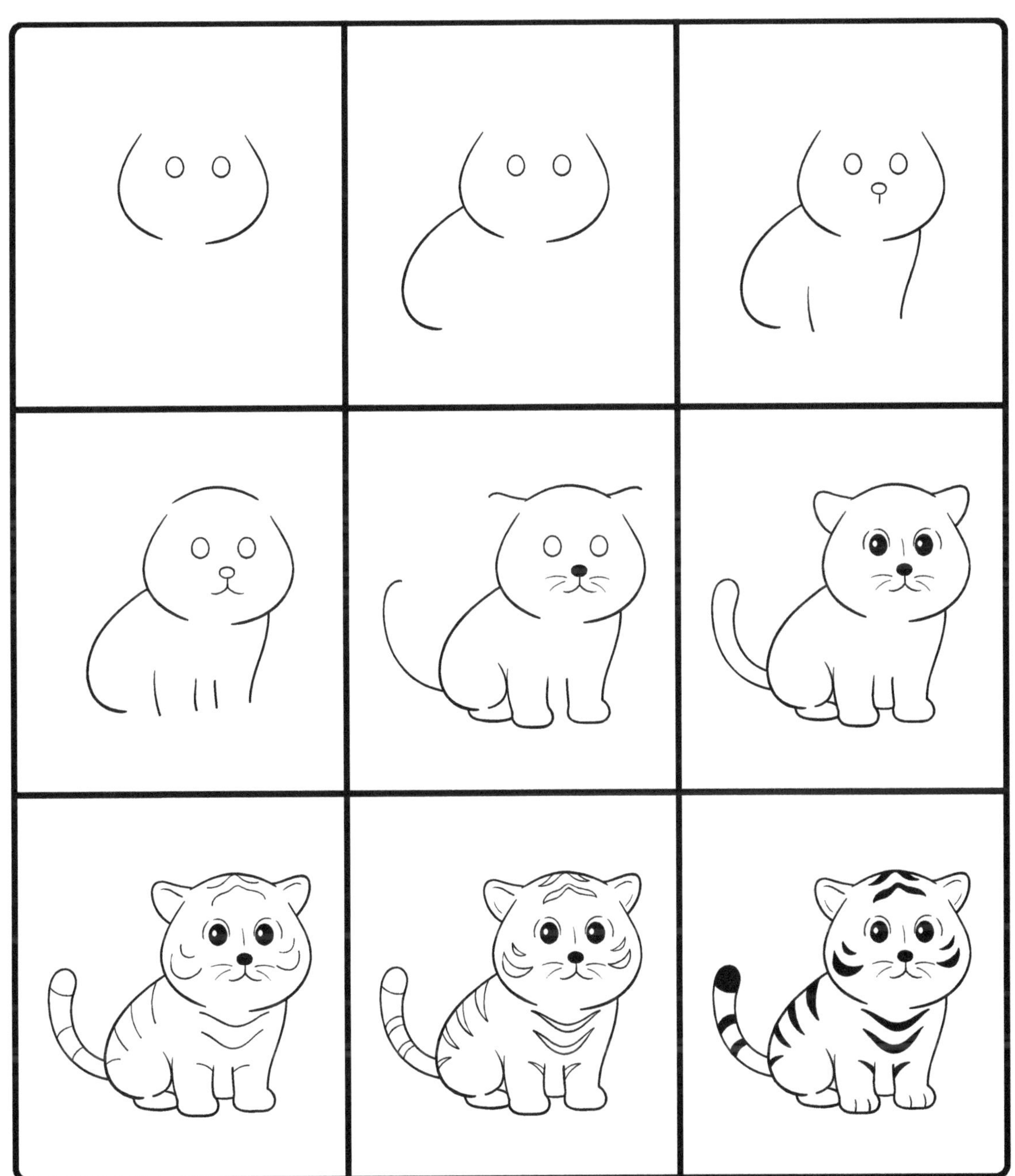

ANTIPODES

LIVES:

IN A ZOO IN ENGLAND.

LOVES:

ELEPHANTS, BUT THEIR HUGS ARE TOO TIGHT!

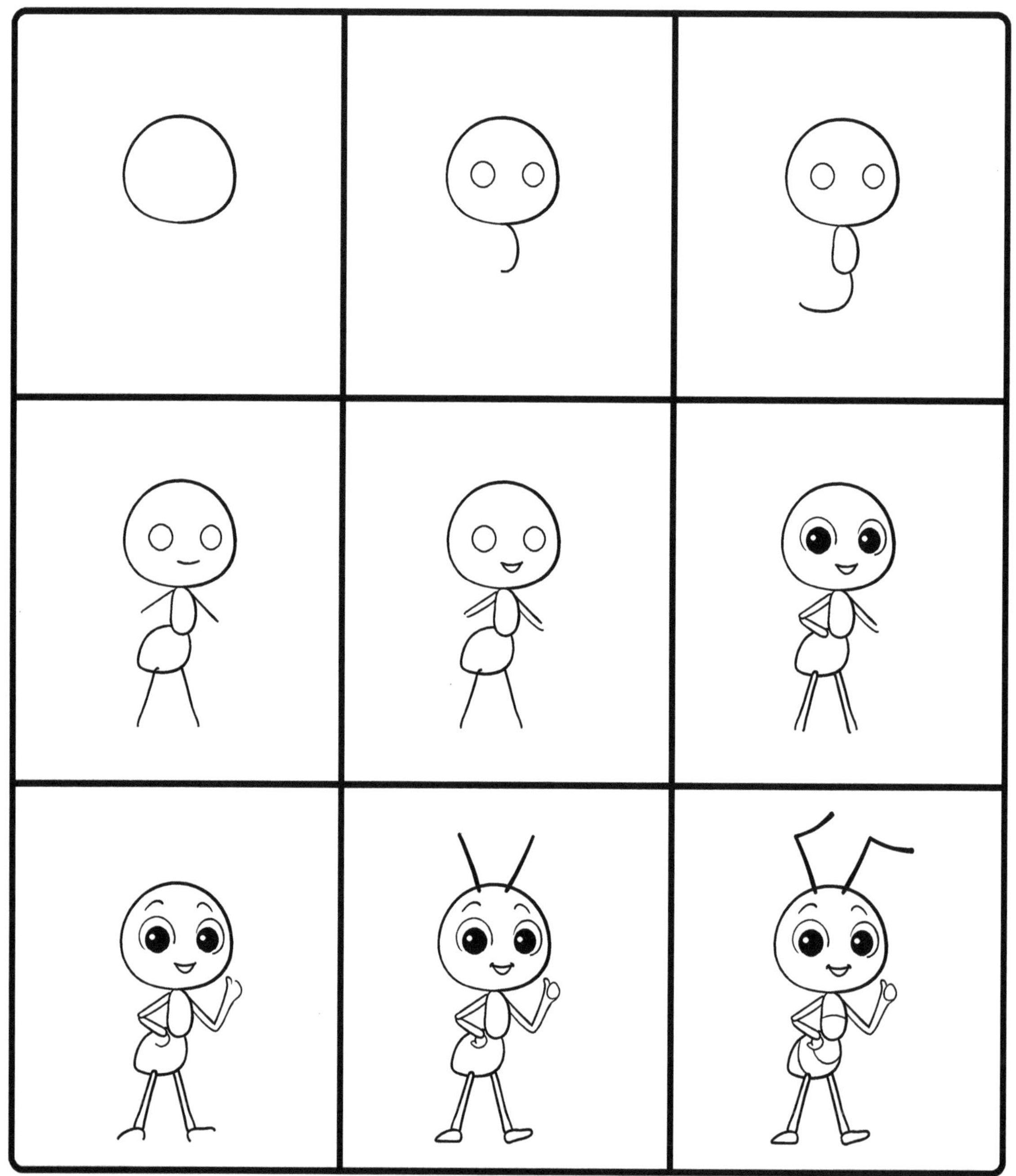

SNIG

LIVES:

IN A MUDDY PIGSTY.

LOVES:

CHOCOLATE. IT LOOKS A LOT LIKE MUD, BUT THAT TASTE; UGH!

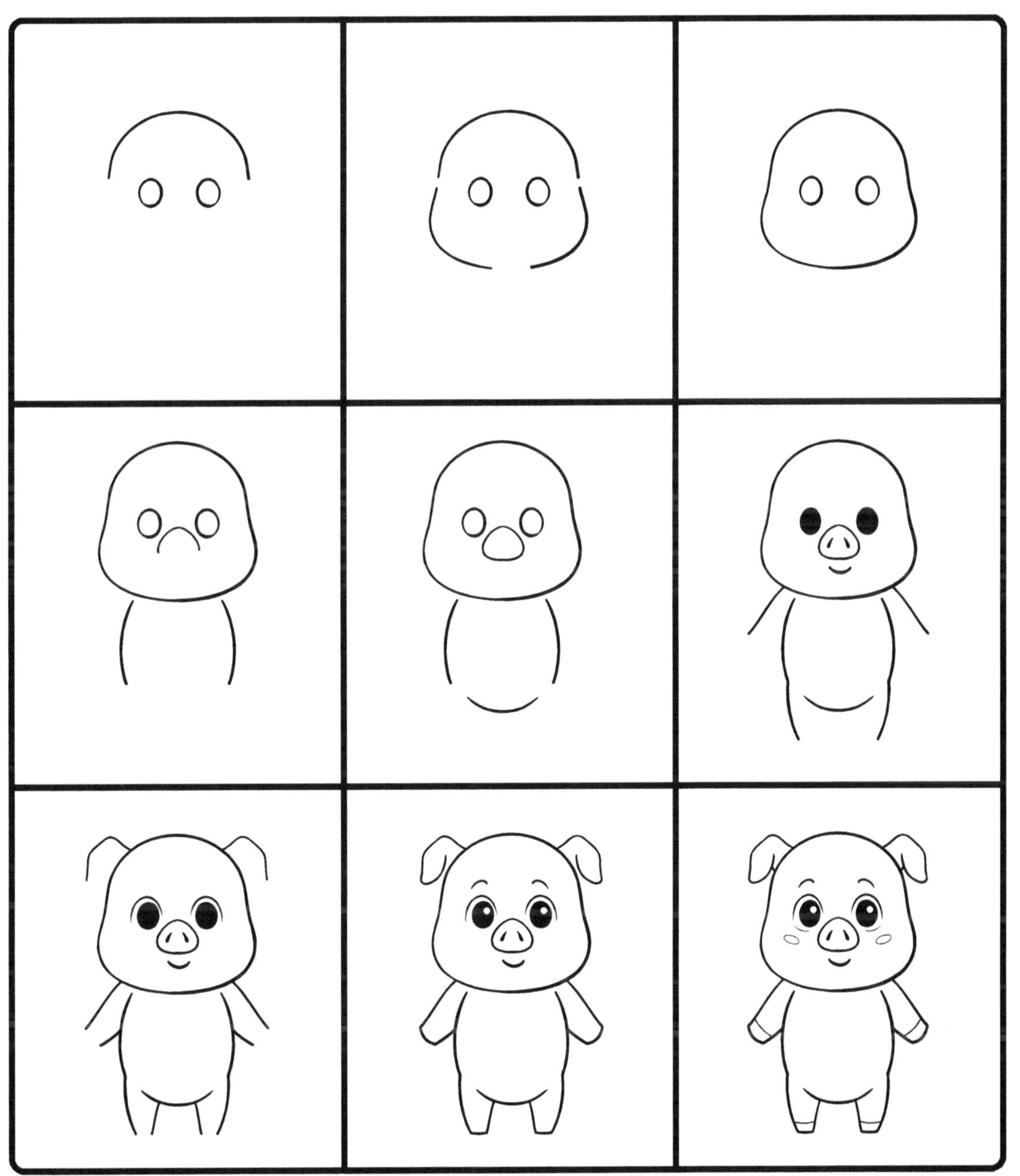

SPEEDY

LIVES:

IN A COTTAGE GARDEN.

LOVES:

LOVES RACING COMPETITIONS, BUT ALWAYS COMES LAST.

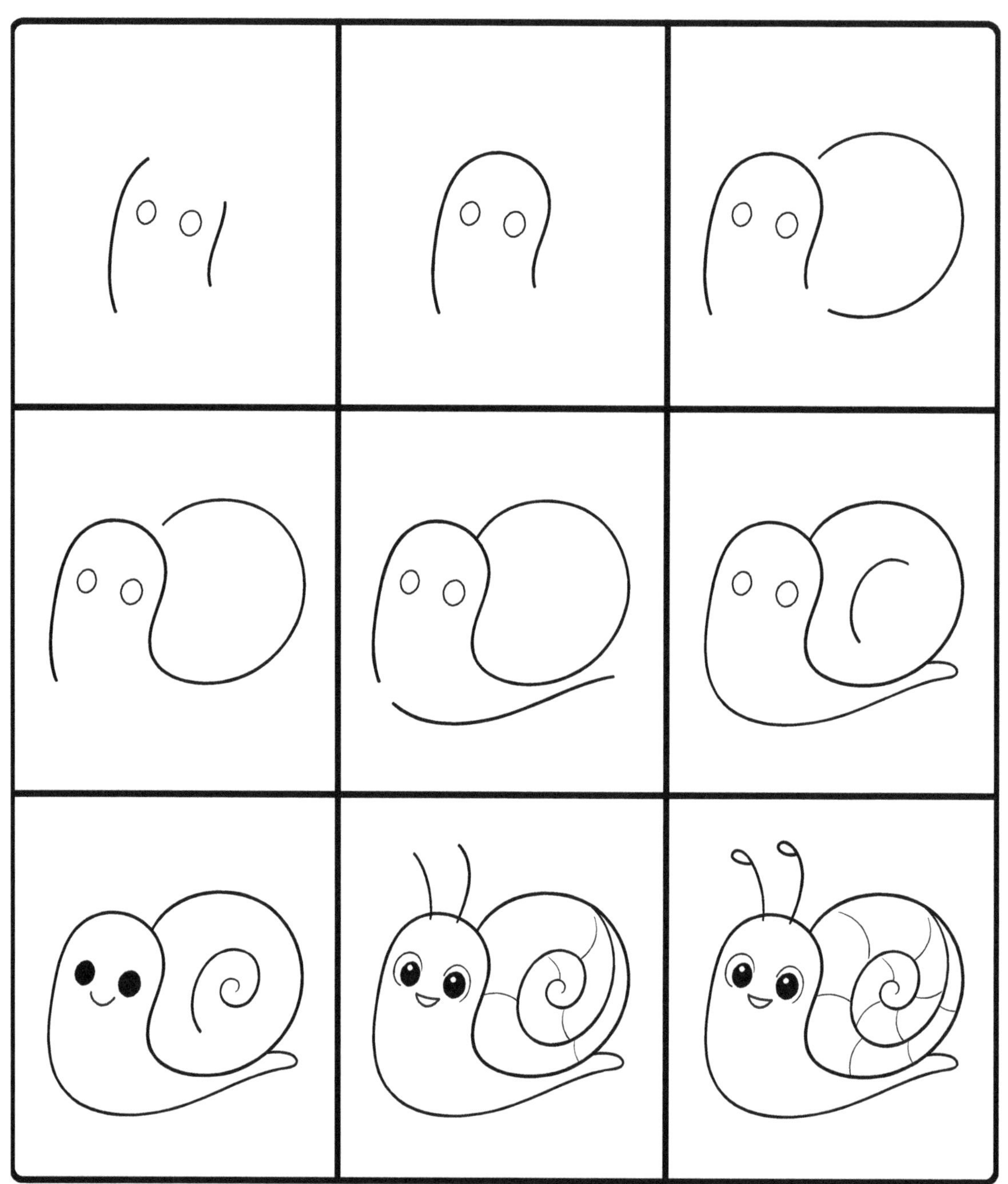

RATTUS

LIVES:

IN A HOLE IN THE WALL OF A FANCY HOUSE.

LOVES:

PLAYING DRESS UPS TO SCARE THE CAT!

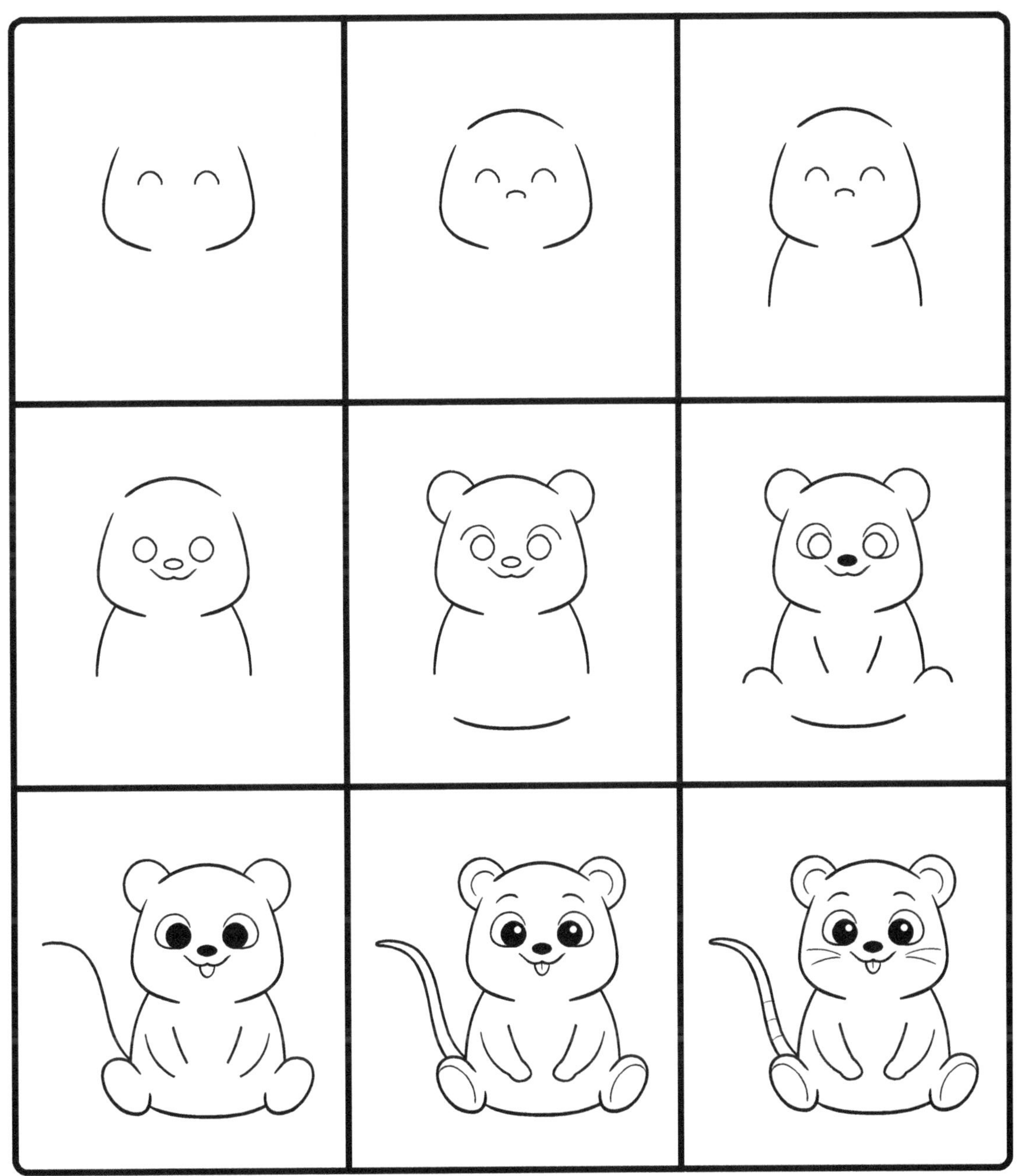

SQUISH

LIVES:

ON THE OUTSKIRTS OF A COUNTRY TOWN.

LOVES:

TO BE CUDDLED AND TOLD, 'OH YOU'RE SO CUTE!' BUT THE TEDDY BEARS GET ALL THE ATTENTION.

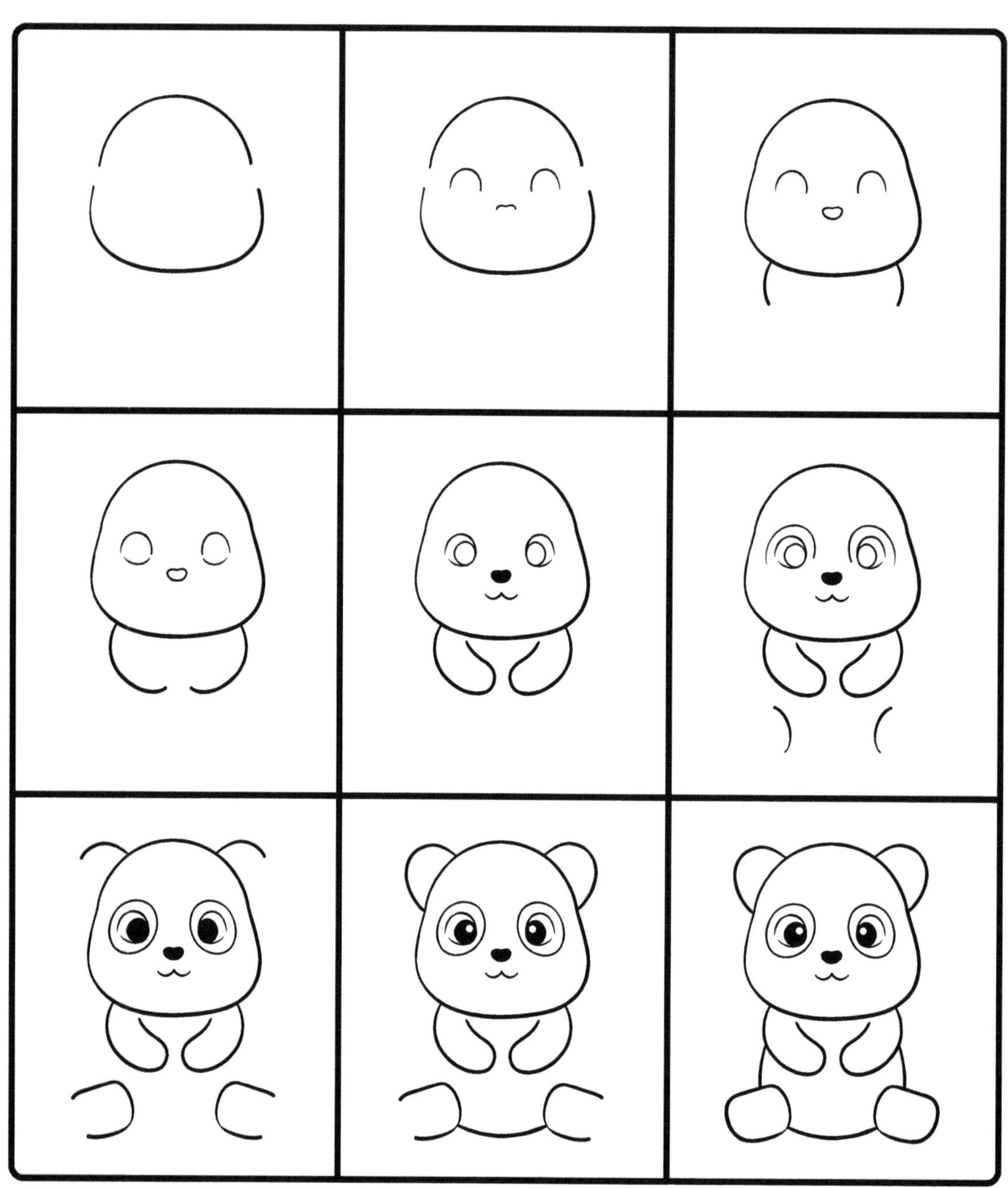

DOTTY

LIVES:

BESIDE A POPULAR HIKING TRAIL.

LOVES:

TO GIVE AND GET HUGS, BUT KIDS ARE A LITTLE SCARED.

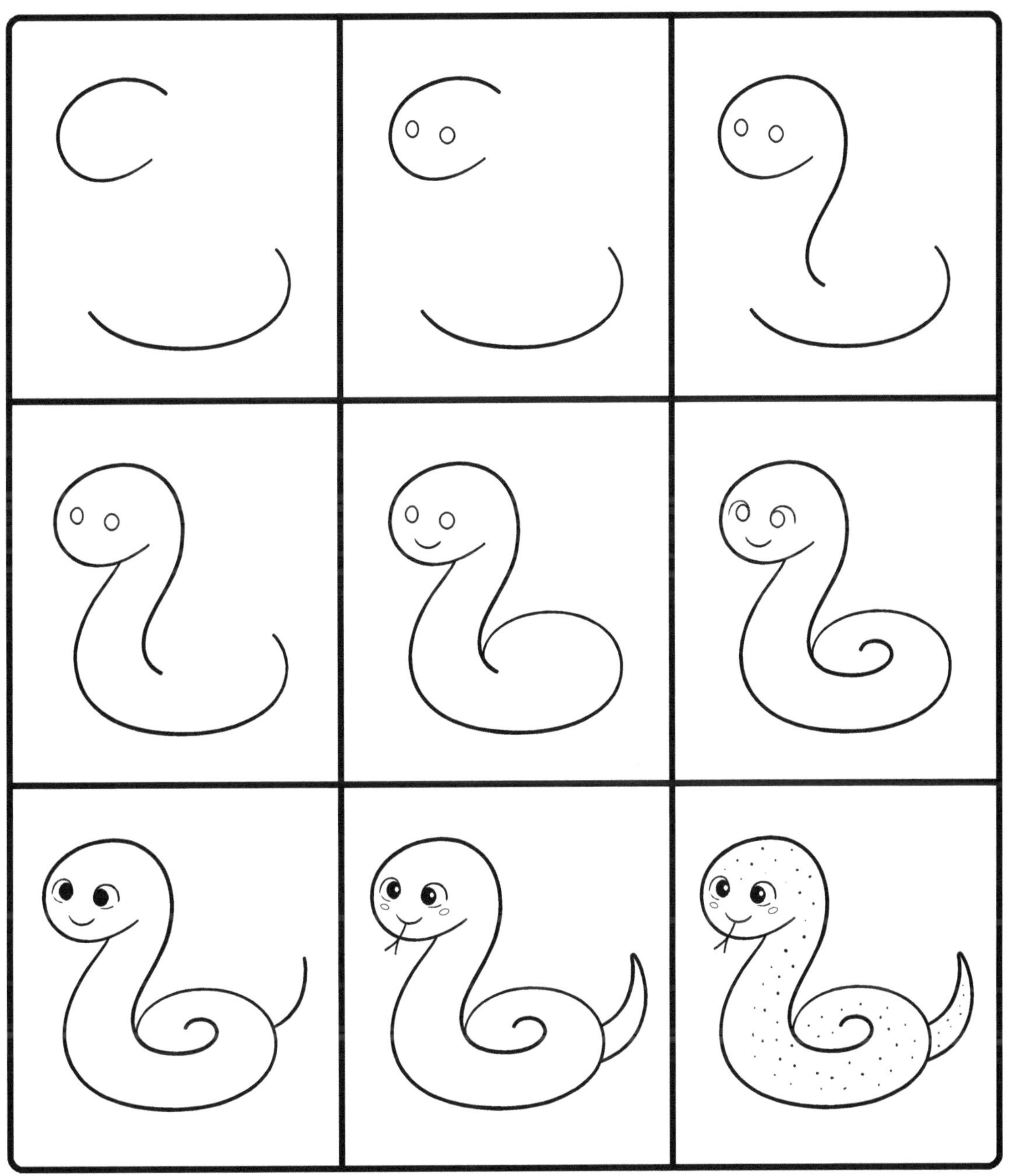

MONKEM

LIVES:

IN BALI, AT A POPULAR TEMPLE.

LOVES:

SWIPING THINGS FROM TOURISTS.

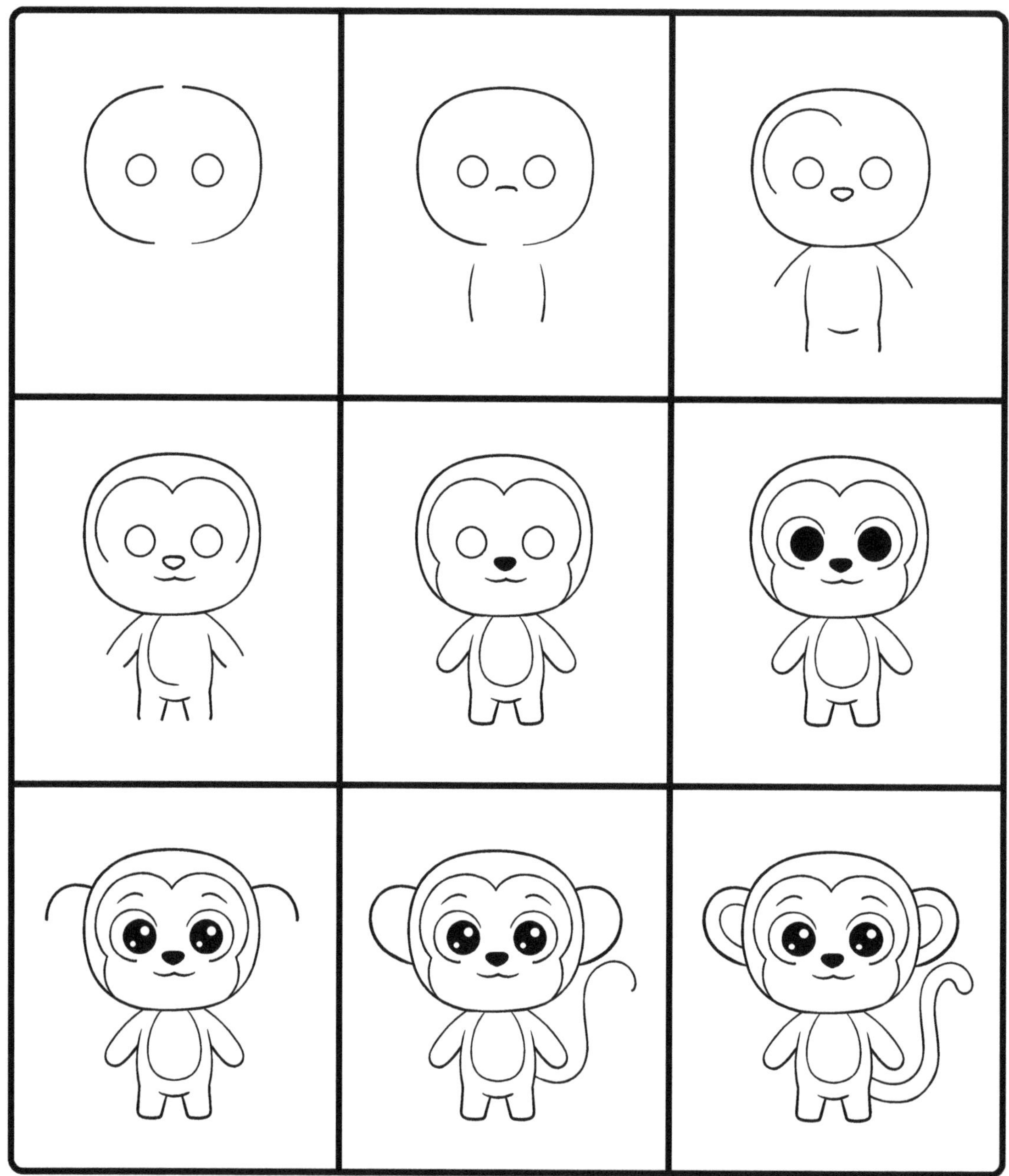

MOOGIE

LIVES:

ON A FARM IN THE AUSTRALIAN COUNTRYSIDE.

LOVES:

PLAYING WITH THE SHEEPDOGS.

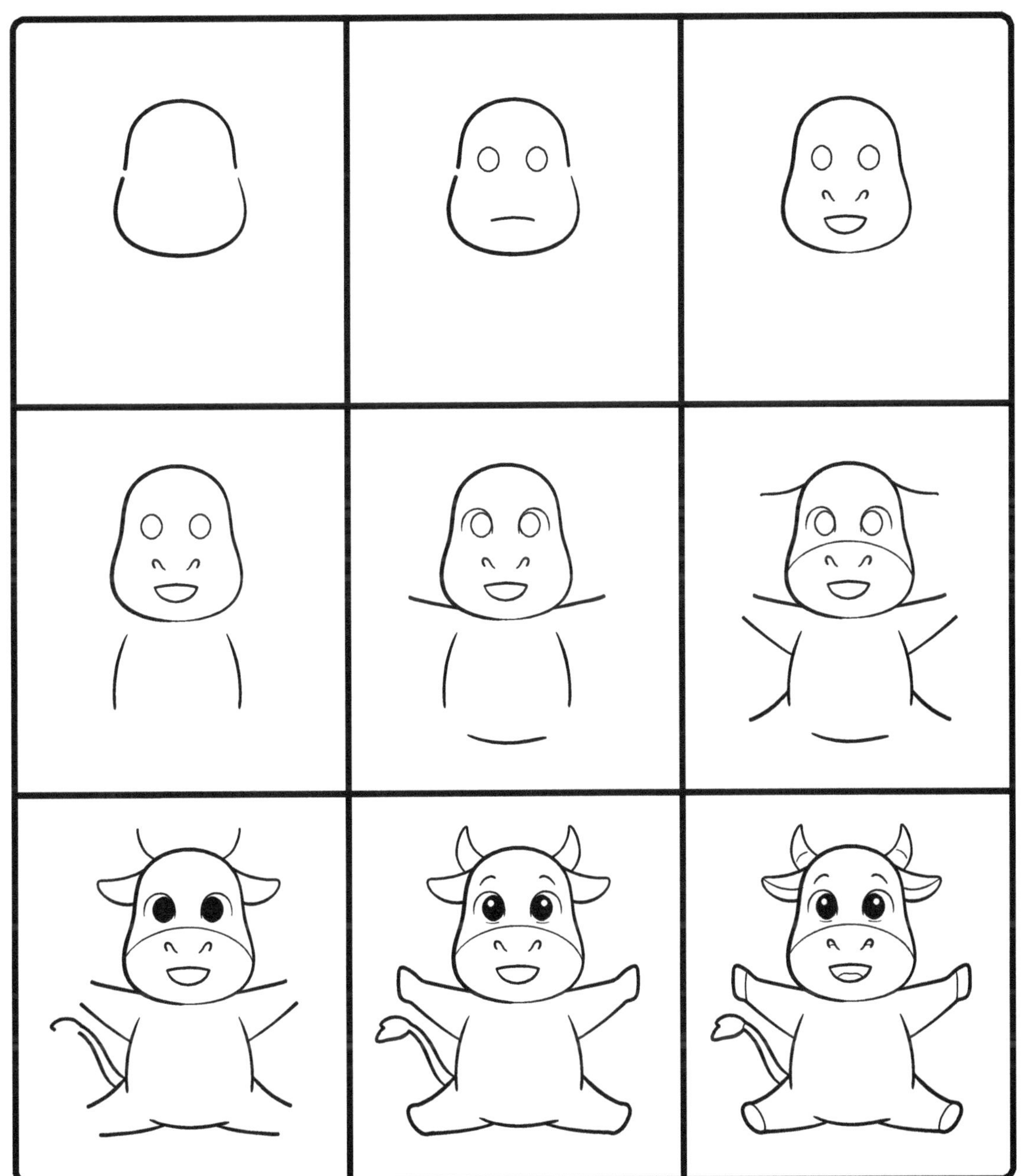

FINNSTER

LIVES:

IN A FISH TANK IN A FANCY HOTEL.

LOVES:

TO WRITE STORIES, AND THE PAPER ALWAYS GETS WET!

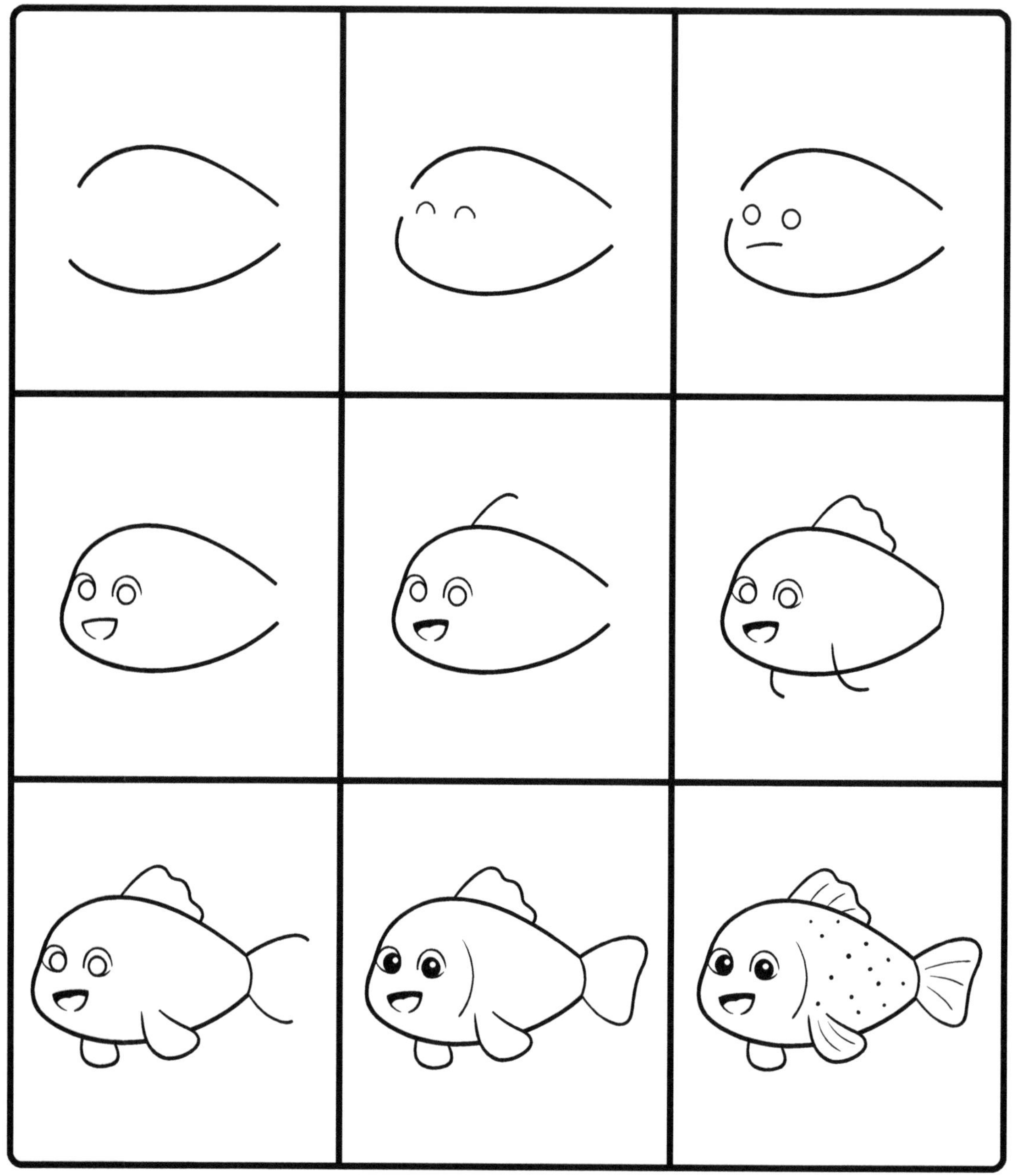

FLAP

LIVES:

AT THE TOP OF A TALL, TALL TREE.

LOVES:

TO FLY WITH THE SUN ON ITS WINGS, BUT IS ALWAYS ASLEEP IN THE DAY.

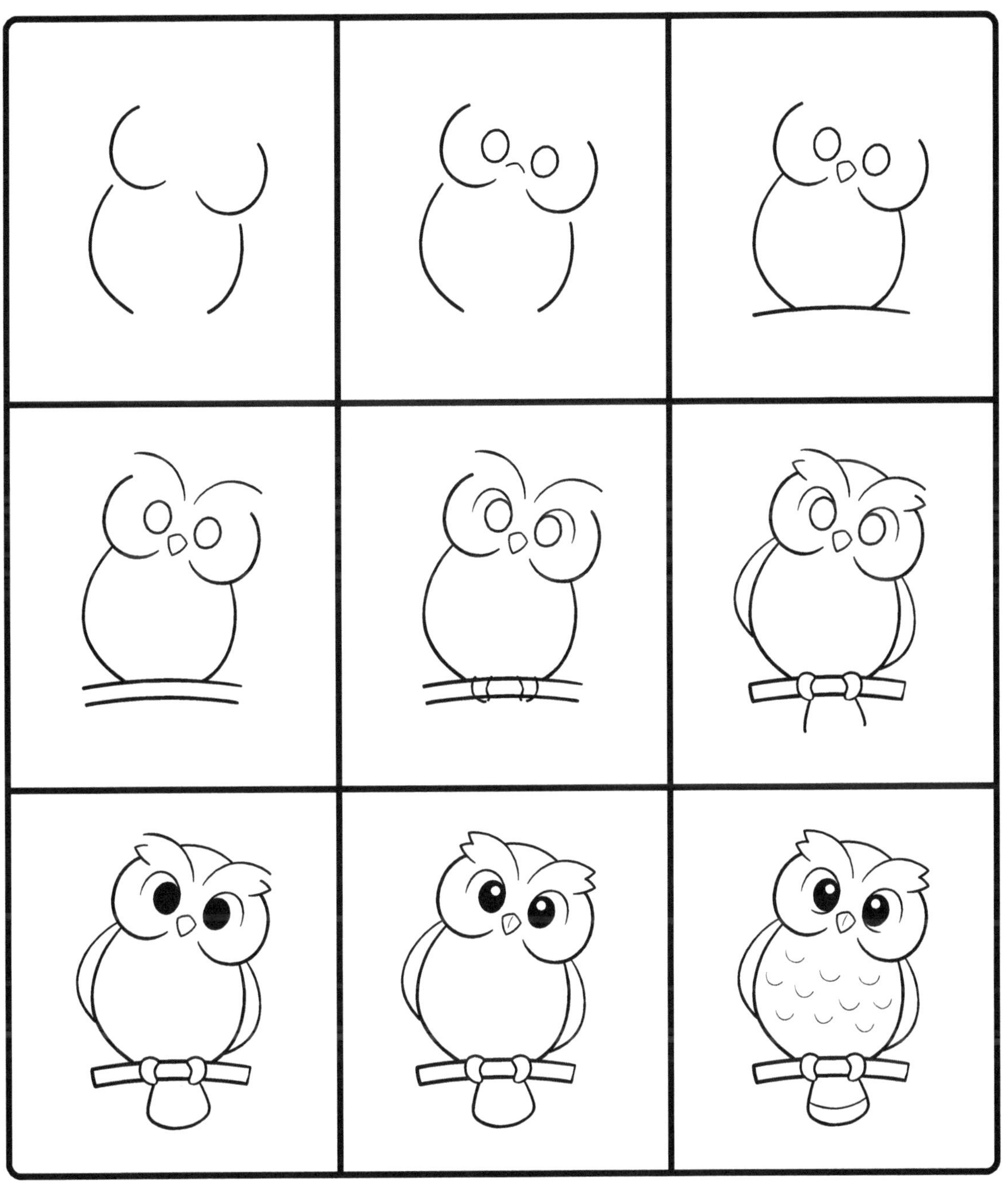

SAURY

LIVES:

ONLY IN BOOKS!

LOVES:

HAVING HIS SKELETON ON SHOW IN MUSEUMS AROUND THE WORLD.

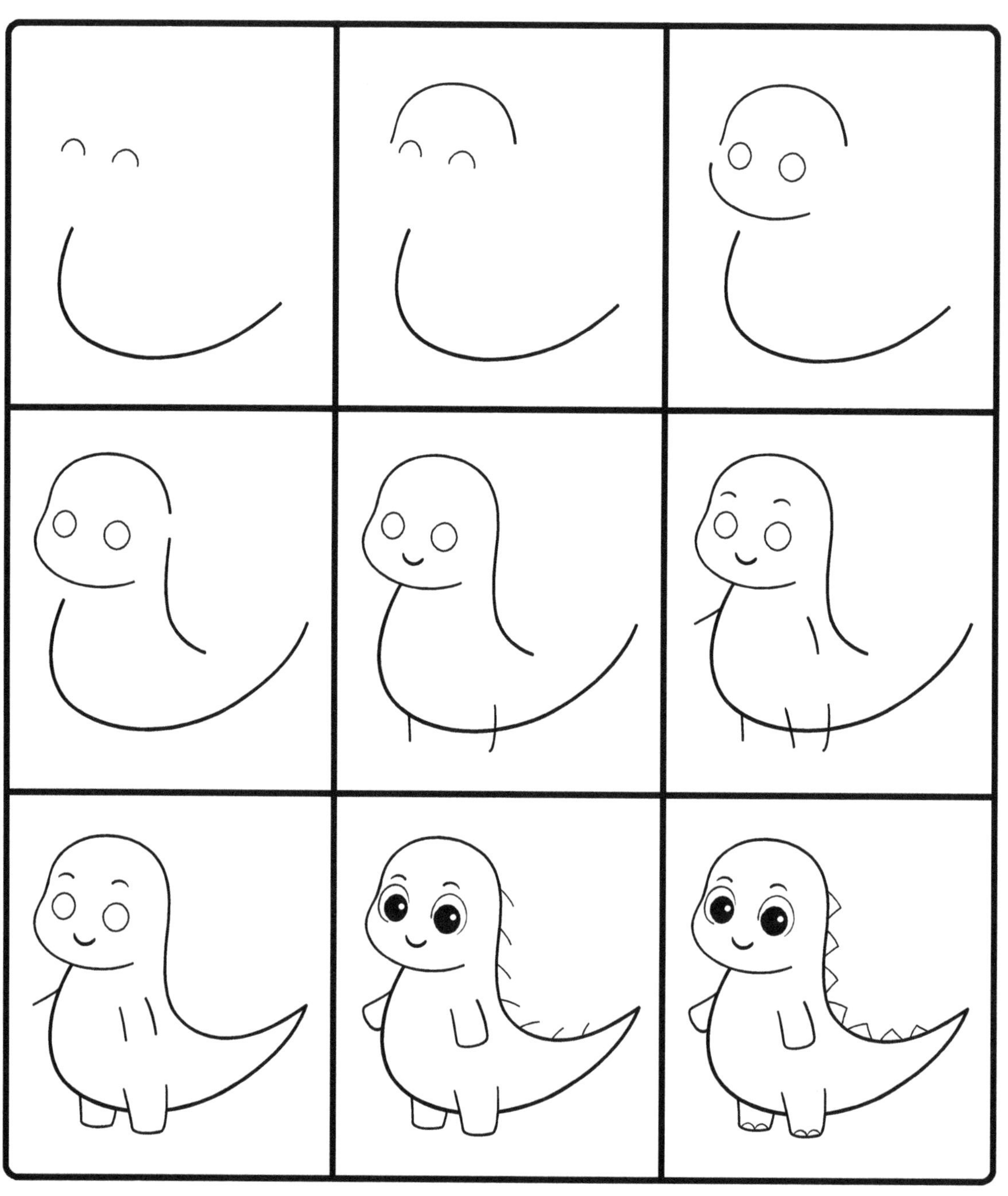

FLIT

LIVES:

ON THE EDGES OF A MAPLE FOREST.

LOVES:

AUTUMN, AND FLYING THROUGH THE MAGICAL CHANGING COLORS OF THE LEAVES.

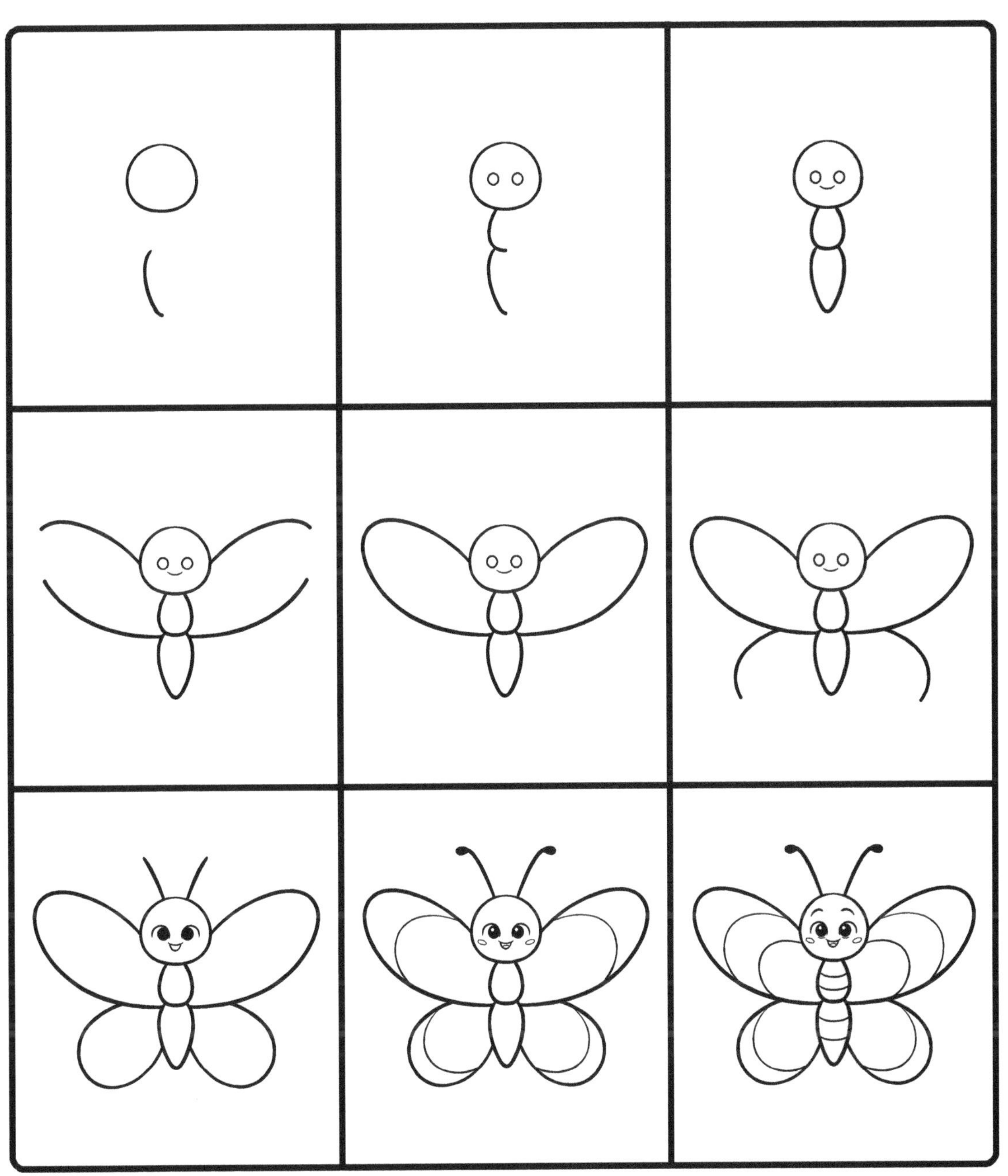

SCAT

LIVES:

WITH HIS SISTER, SKIP.

LOVES:

TO PLAY WITH HIS SISTER, SKIP, BUT HE'S SICK OF DRESS-UPS AND BRACELET-MAKING.

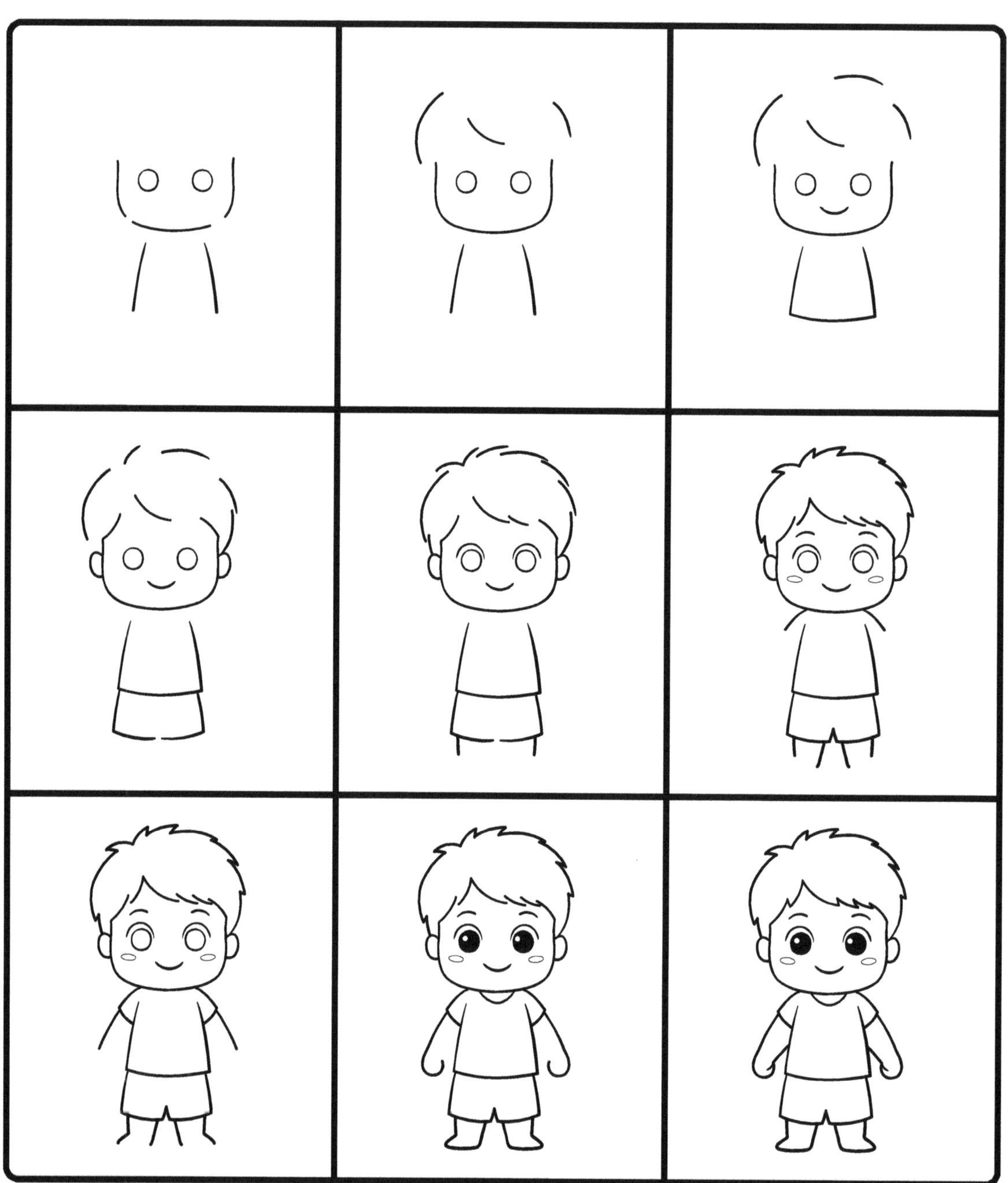

SKIP

LIVES:

WITH HER BROTHER, SCAT.

LOVES:

TO PLAY WITH HER BROTHER, SCAT, BUT SHE'S SICK OF SWORD FIGHTS AND BUG CATCHING.

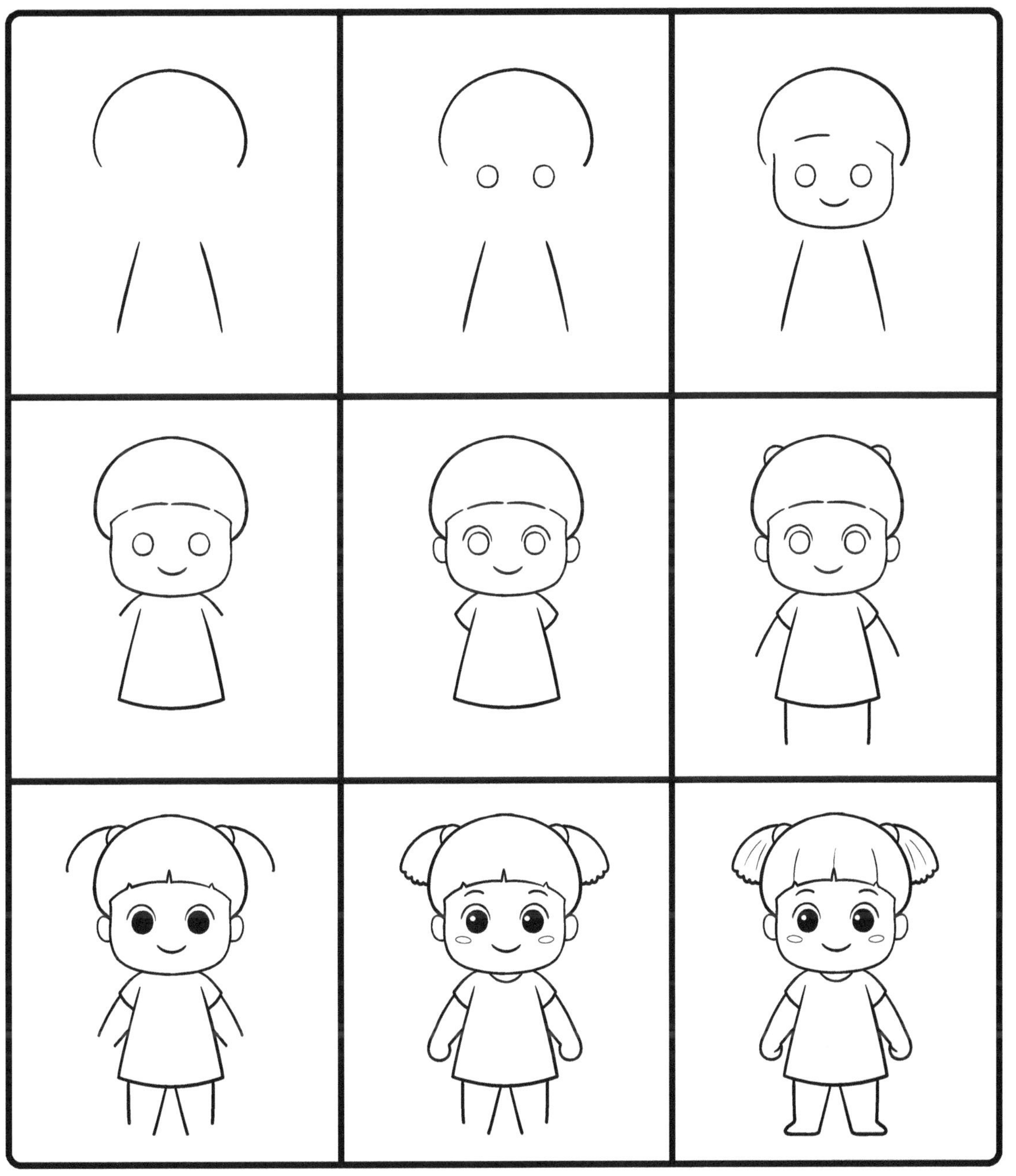

DOLLY

LIVES:

IN DOLPHIN COVE WHERE LOTS OF TOURISTS COME TO PAT HER.

LOVES:

LOVES A PAT, BUT LOVES EVEN MORE THAT SHE IS FREE TO COME AND GO AS SHE PLEASES.

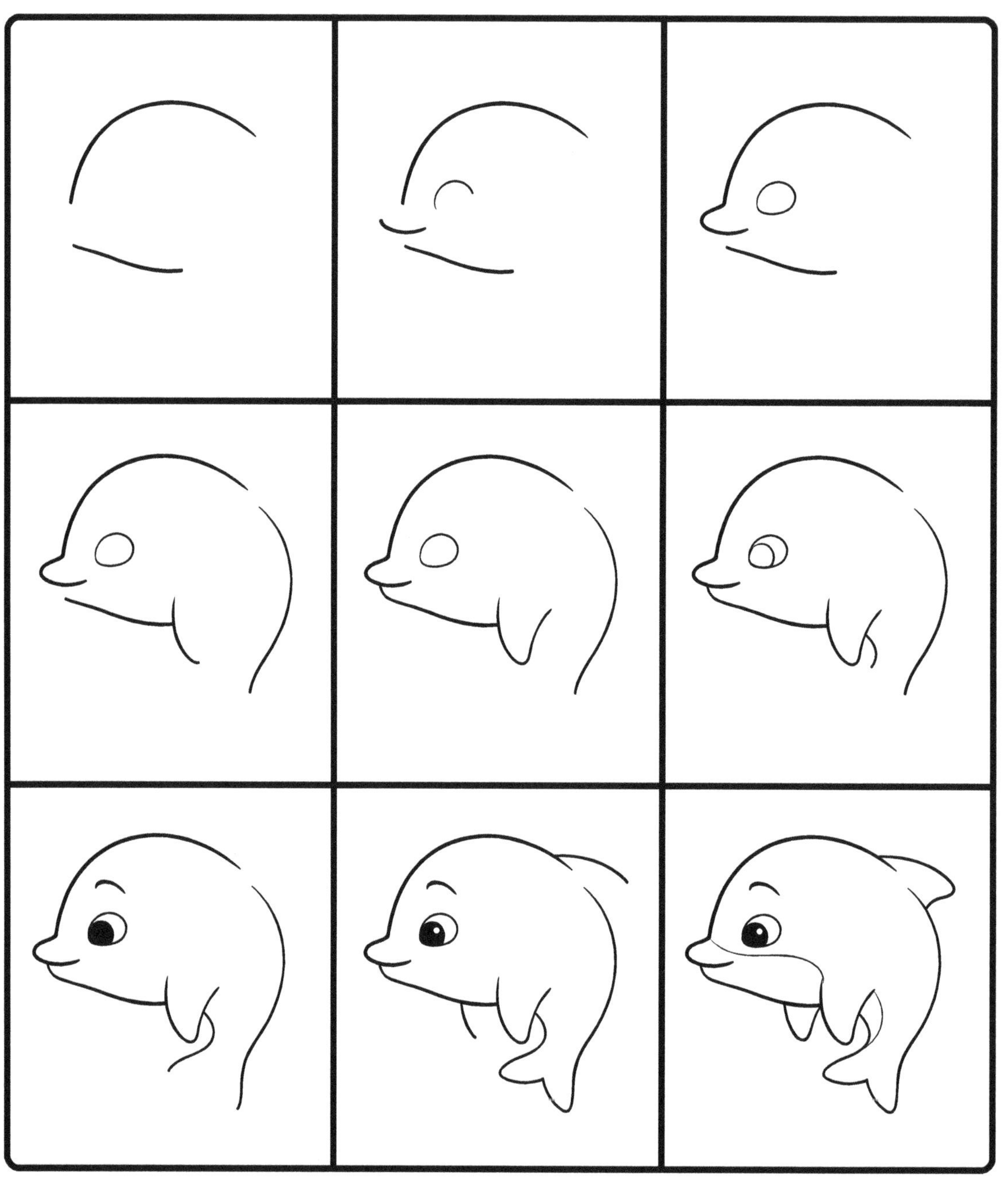

SNUGS

LIVES:

IN A COFFEE SHOP.

LOVES:

PUTTING SMILES ON PEOPLE'S FACES AS THEY TAKE THEIR FIRST SIP.

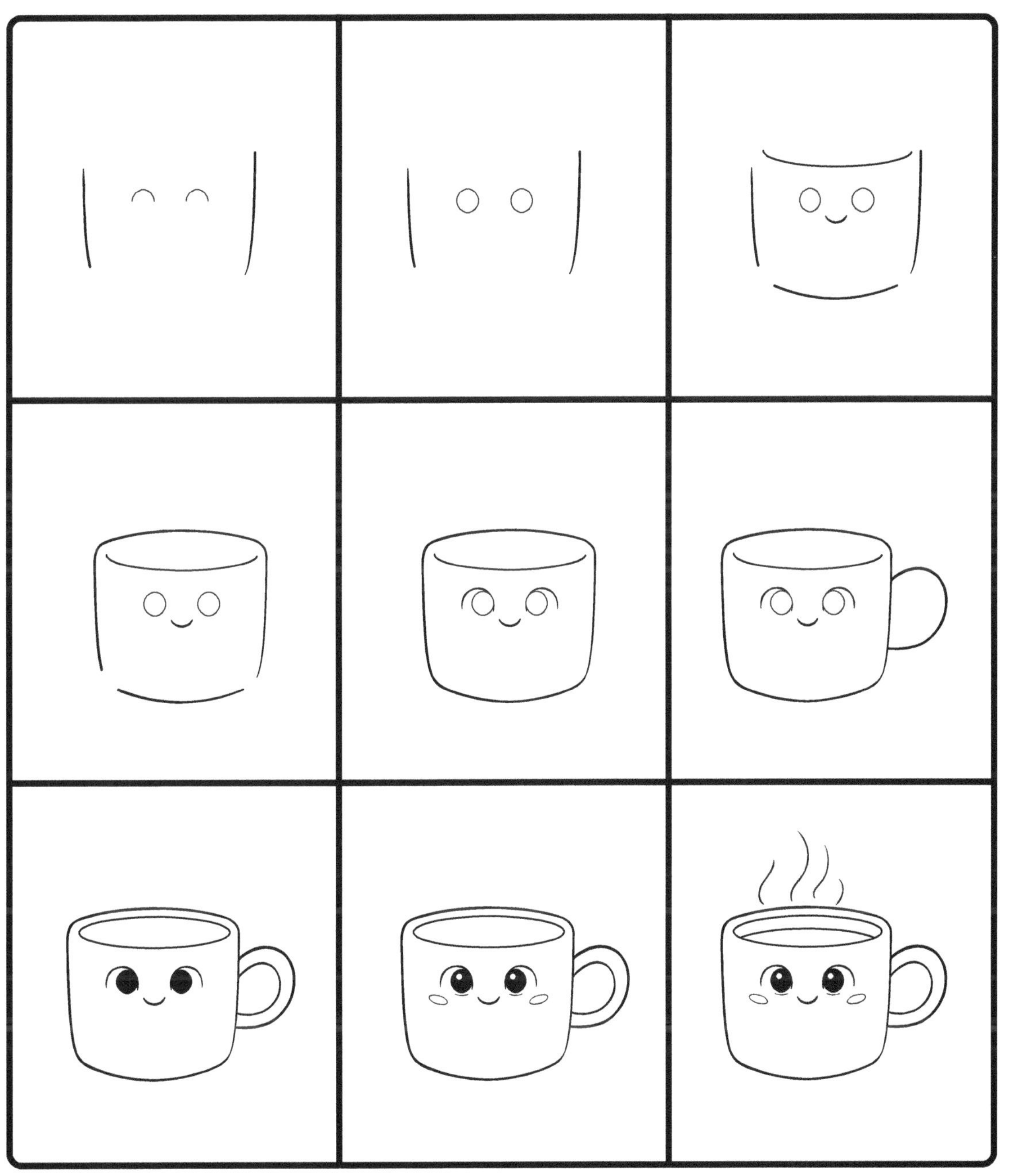

BEAKY

LIVES:

IN A PINE FOREST.

LOVES:

WORMS, BUT HATES HAVING TO GET UP SO EARLY!

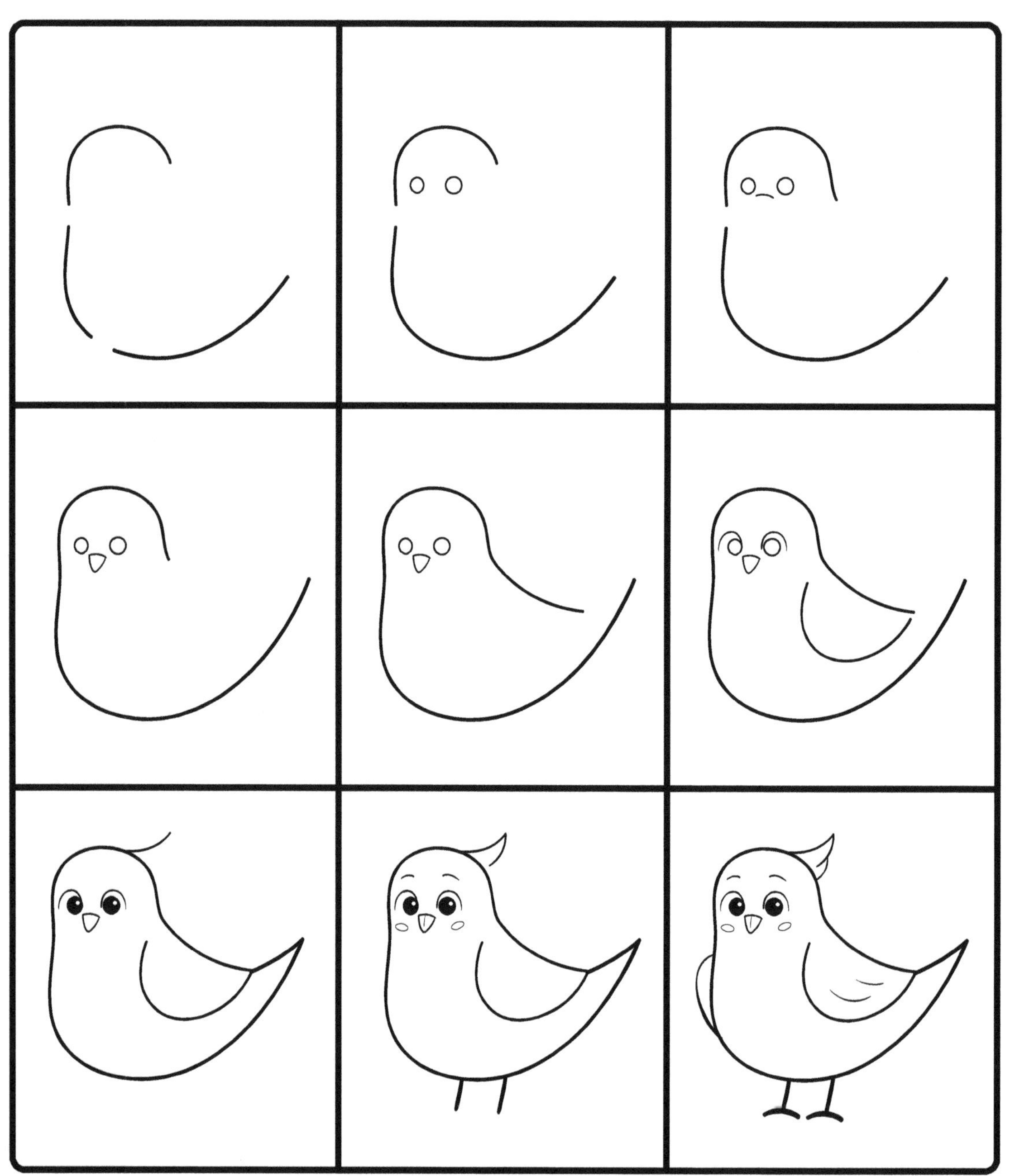

GIRLY

LIVES:

ON A FARM OWNED BY A LOVELY FAMILY.

LOVES:

WAKING UP JUST AS THE SUN STARTS TO SHINE, THEN WAKING EVERYONE ELSE UP!

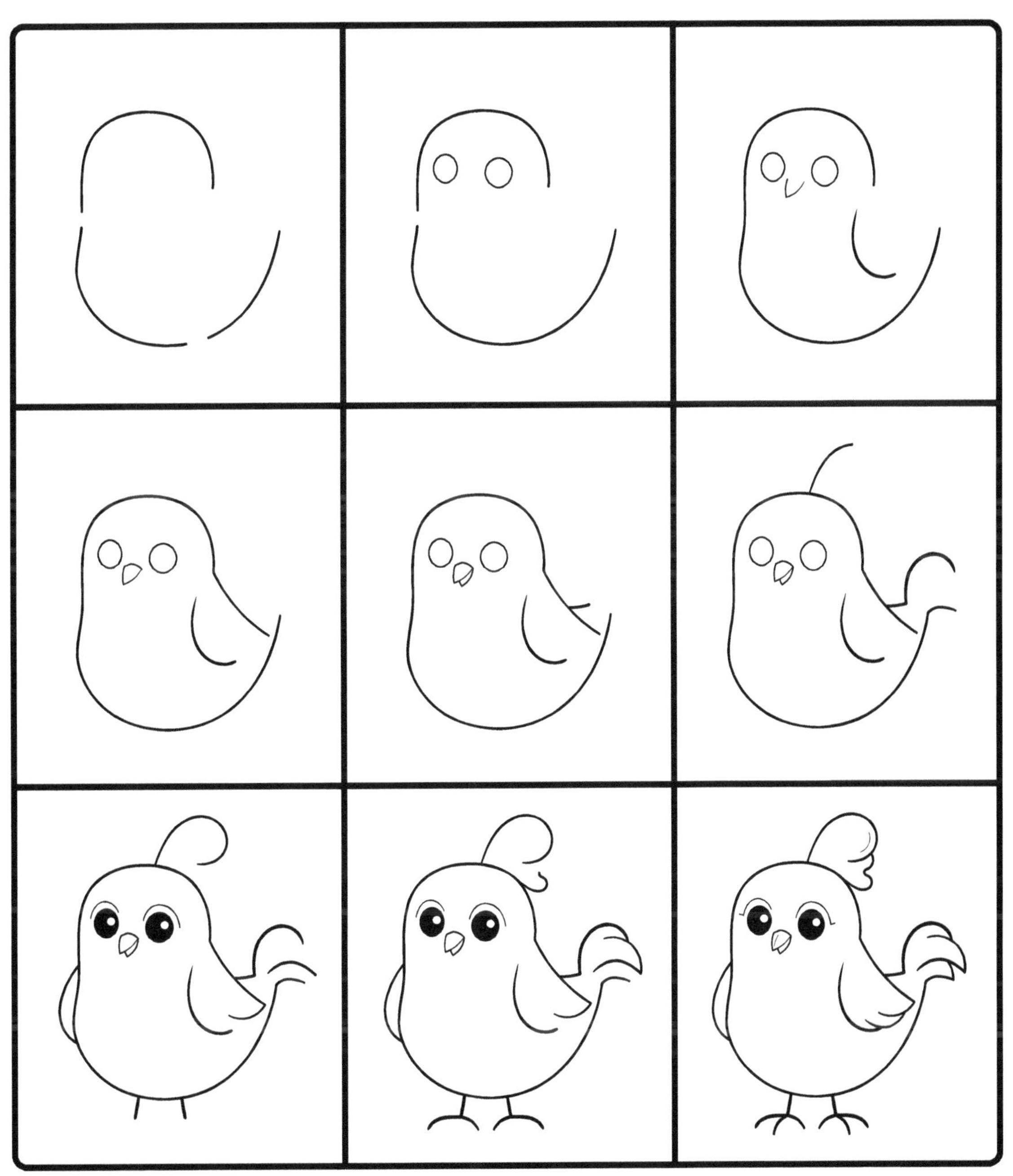

SHELBY

LIVES:

JUST OFF THE COAST OF MIAMI.

LOVES:

TO BREAKDANCE BUT GETS STUCK ON HIS BACK.

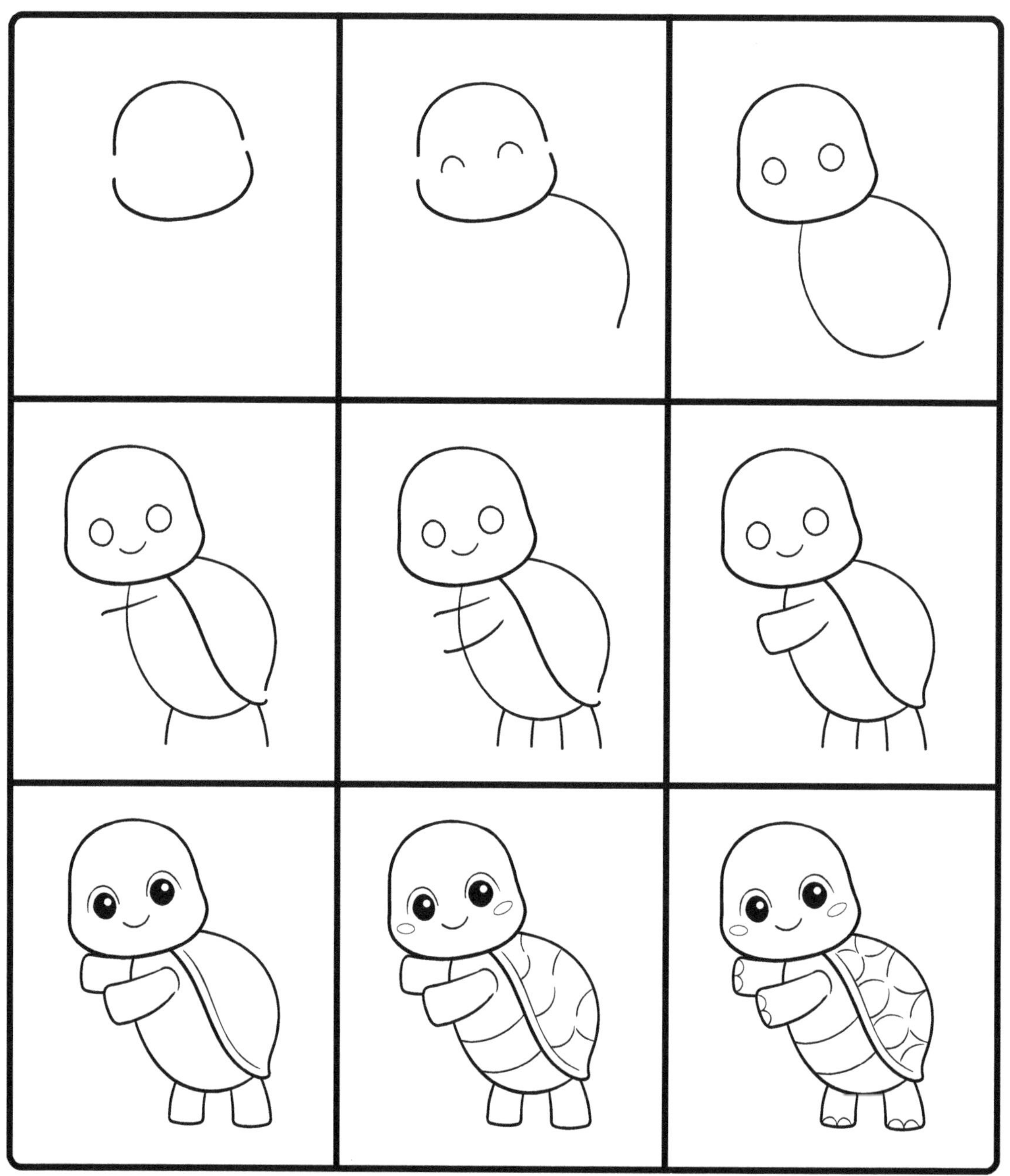

DRIFTER

LIVES:

IN A FRONT YARD, IN FRONT OF THE WINDOW OF A HOME.

LOVES:

A COZY FIREPLACE IN WINTER, WITH A GOOD BOOK... CAN'T STAY FOR LONG THOUGH!

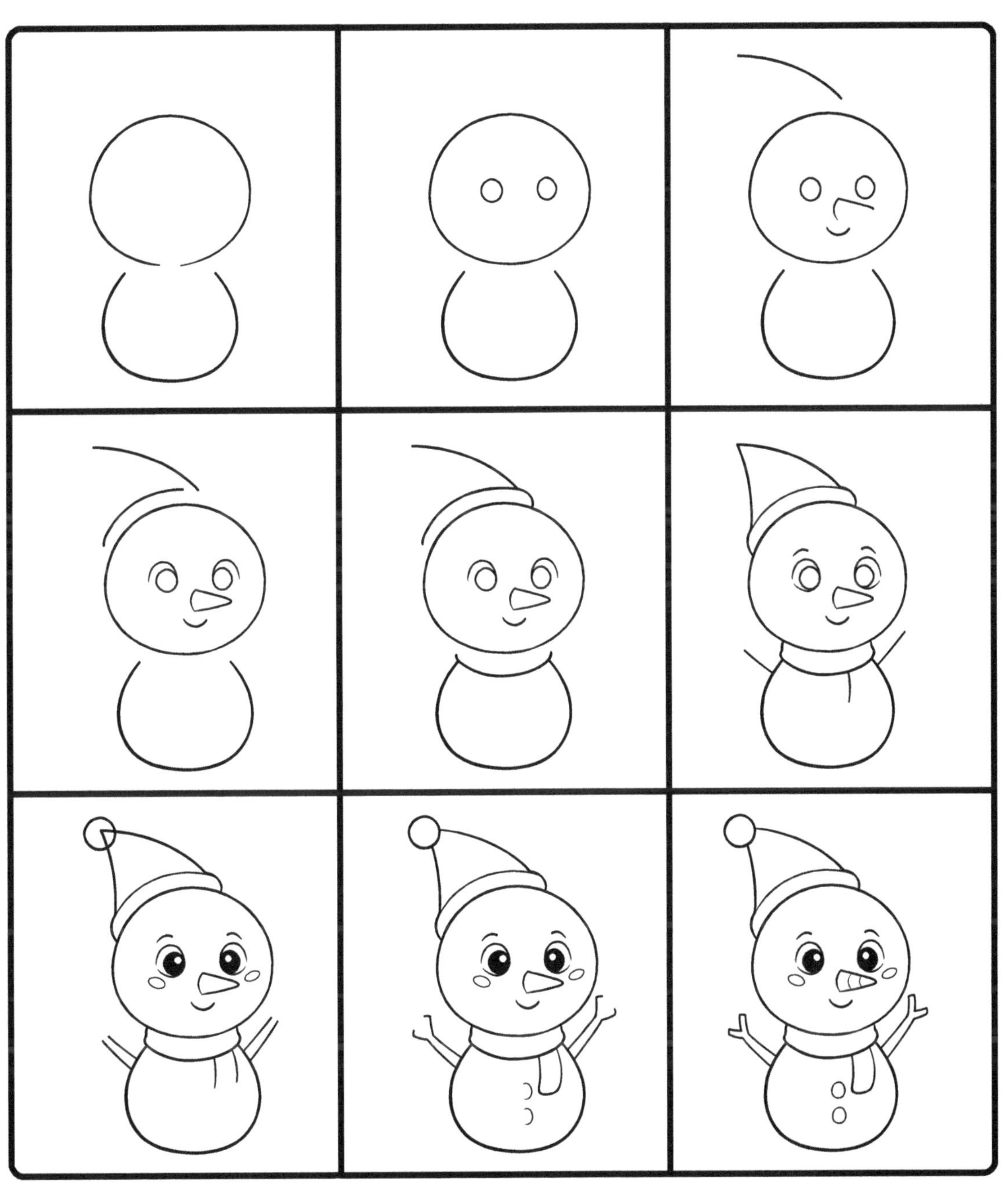

ROB

LIVES:

AT HOME AS A SERVANT AND COOK.

LOVES:

BEING SO CLEVER BUT WOULD LOVE TO KNOW WHAT IT'S LIKE TO BE ALIVE!

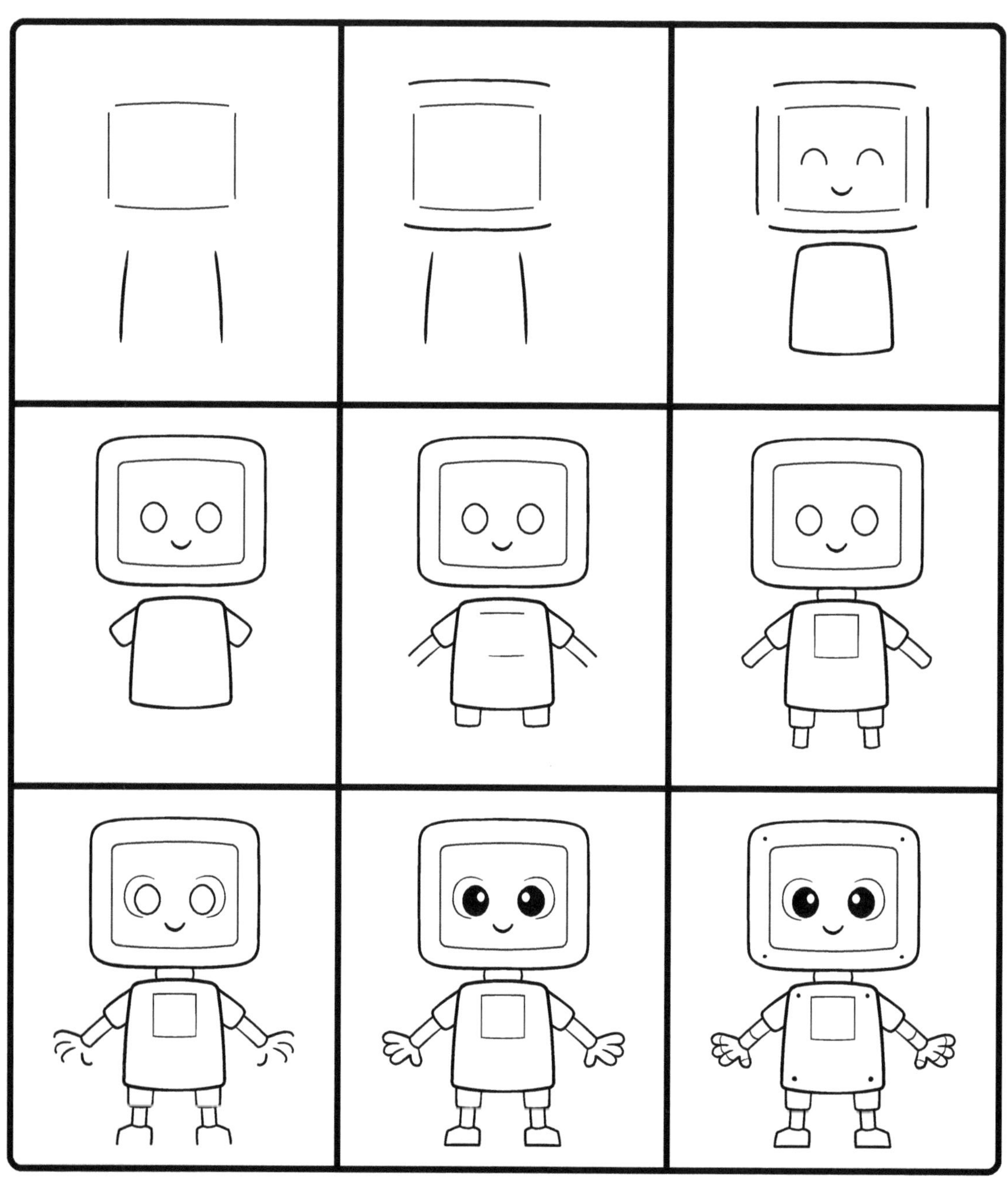

CORN-PIE

LIVES:

ON A SHELF IN A GIRL'S BEDROOM.

LOVES:

POPPING BUBBLE-WRAP WITH ITS HORN.

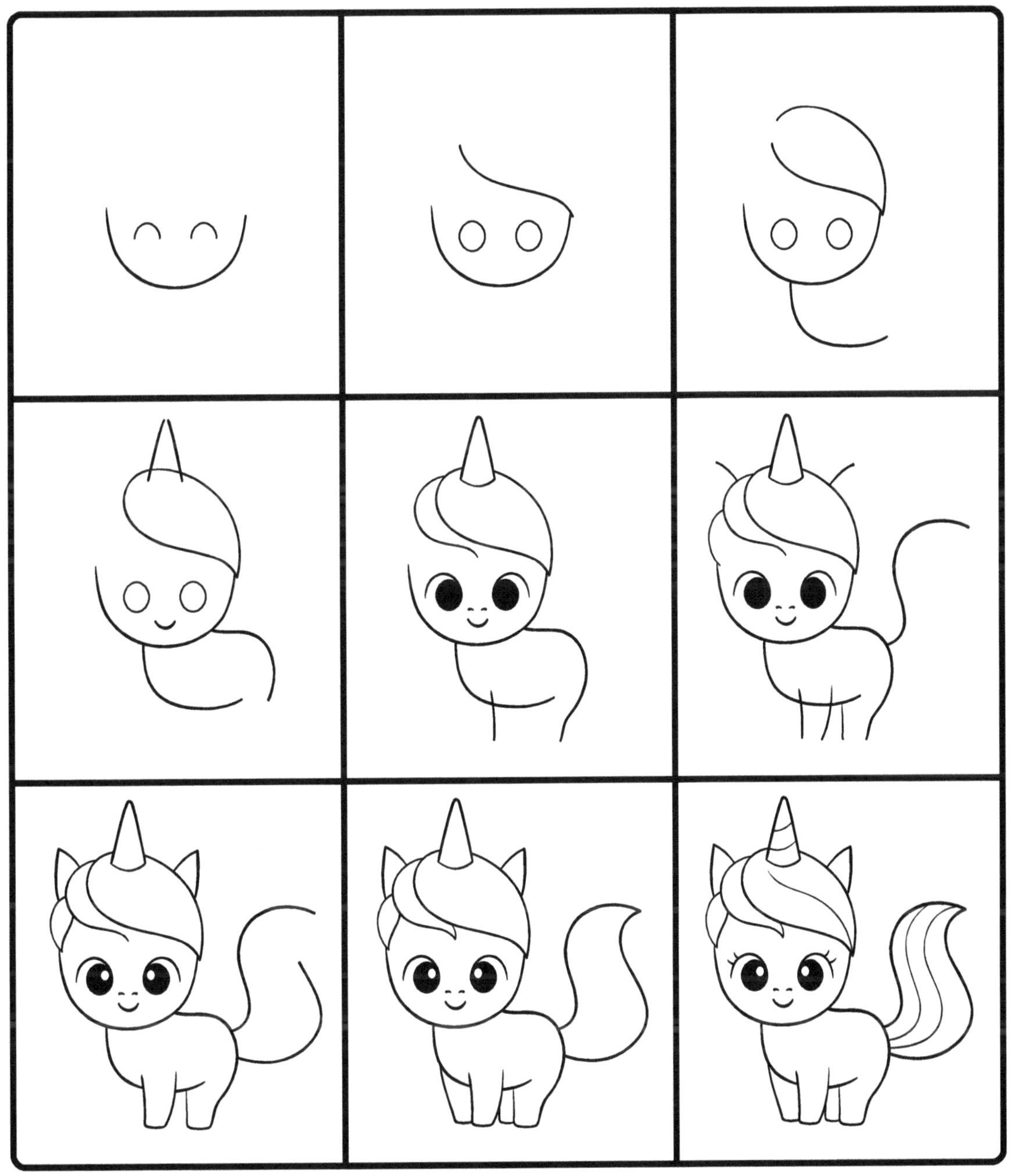

MILKO

LIVES:

IN A FAMILY'S FRIDGE.

LOVES:

WHEN KIDS FLAVOR HIM WITH STRAWBERRY, BUT NOT BANANA, UGH!

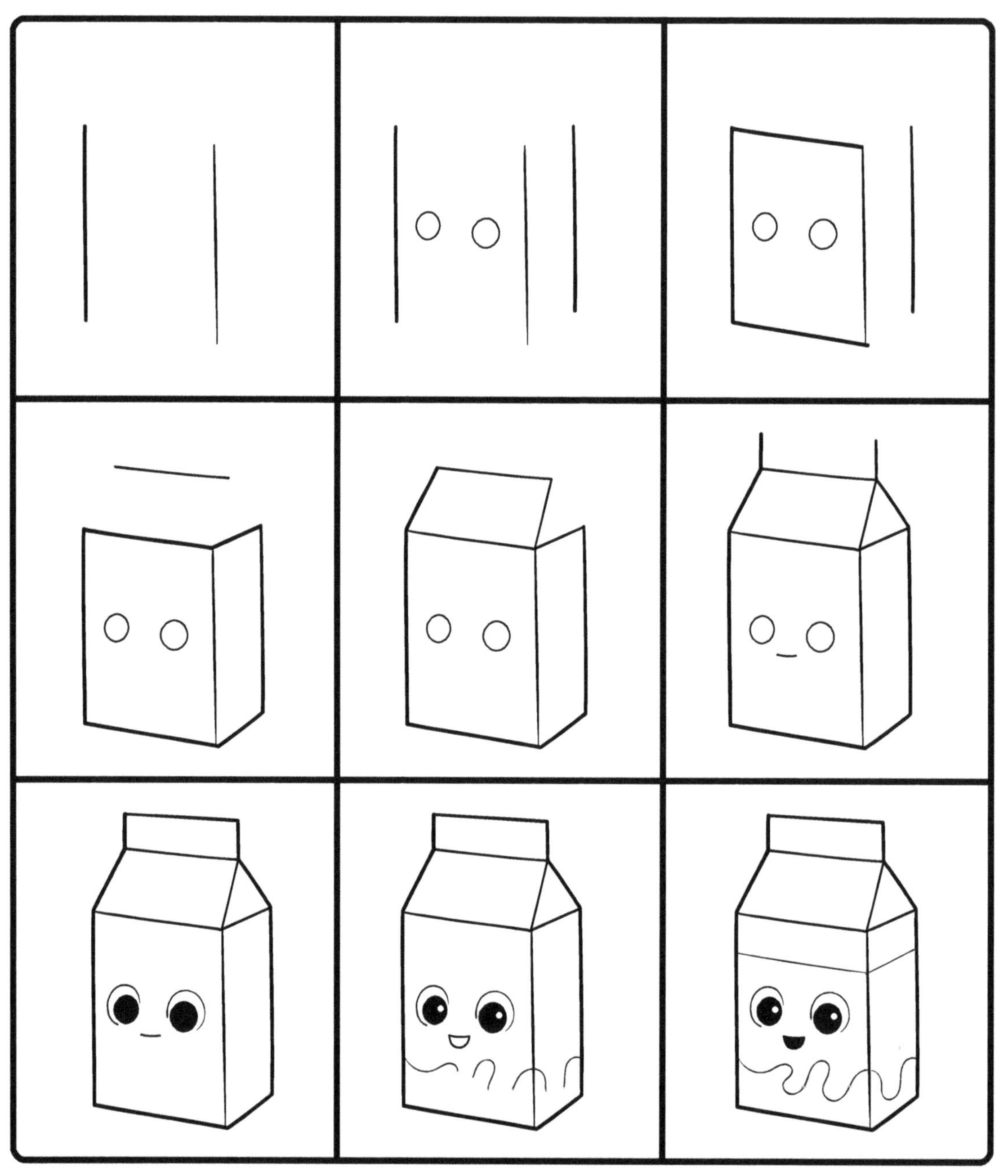

BOTTBEE

LIVES:

AT THE SUPERMARKET.

LOVES:

THE THOUGHT OF BEING RECYCLED ONE DAY. BUT INTO A BIRD FEEDER OR A PLANT POT, NOT FLATTENED AND SQUISHED UP!

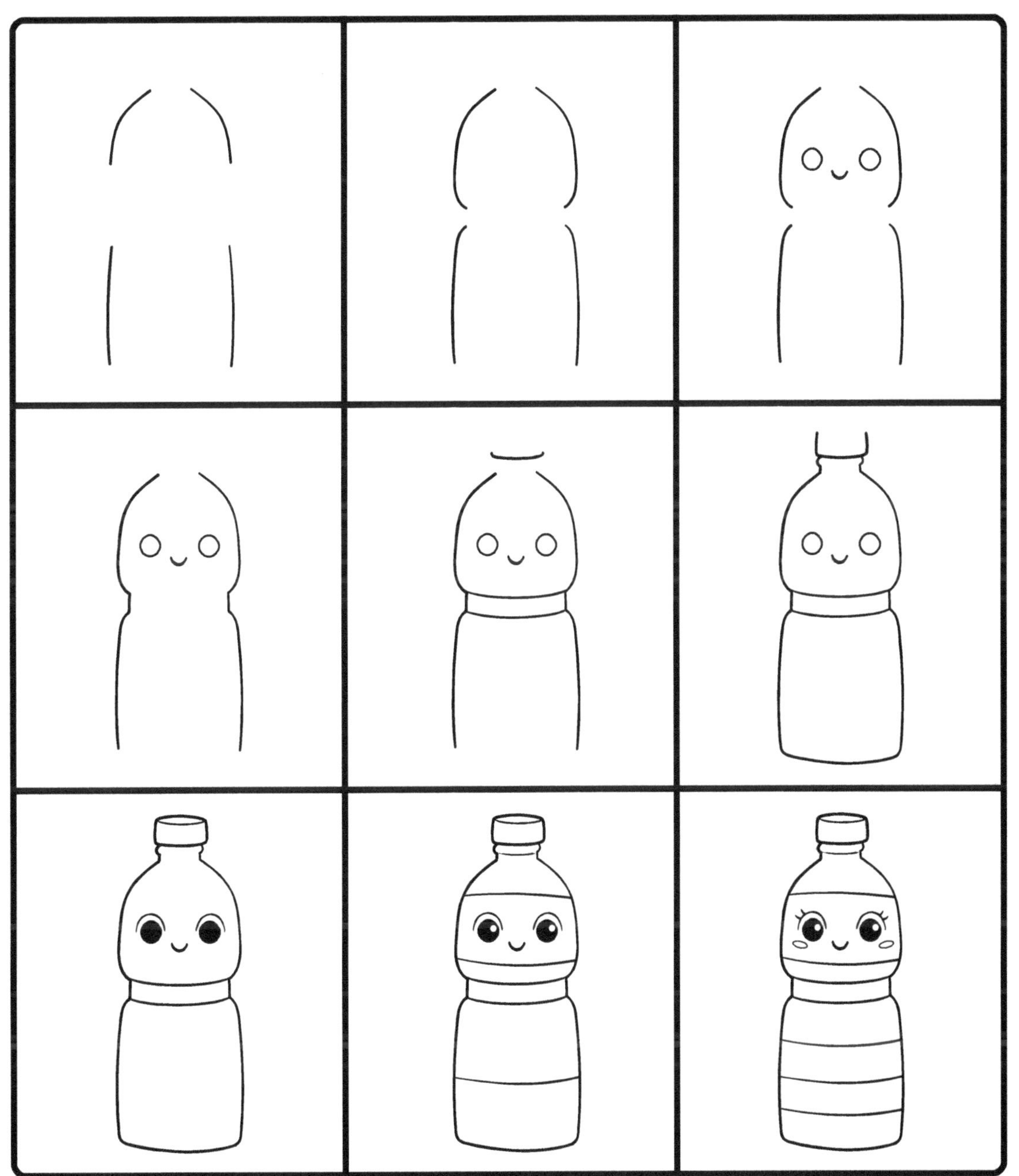

SPRITE

LIVES:

IN A GARDEN, OFTEN PASSED BY KIDS ON THEIR WAY TO SCHOOL.

LOVES:

BEING BEAUTIFUL AND LIVING A LONG GREEN LIFE - DON'T PICK HER!

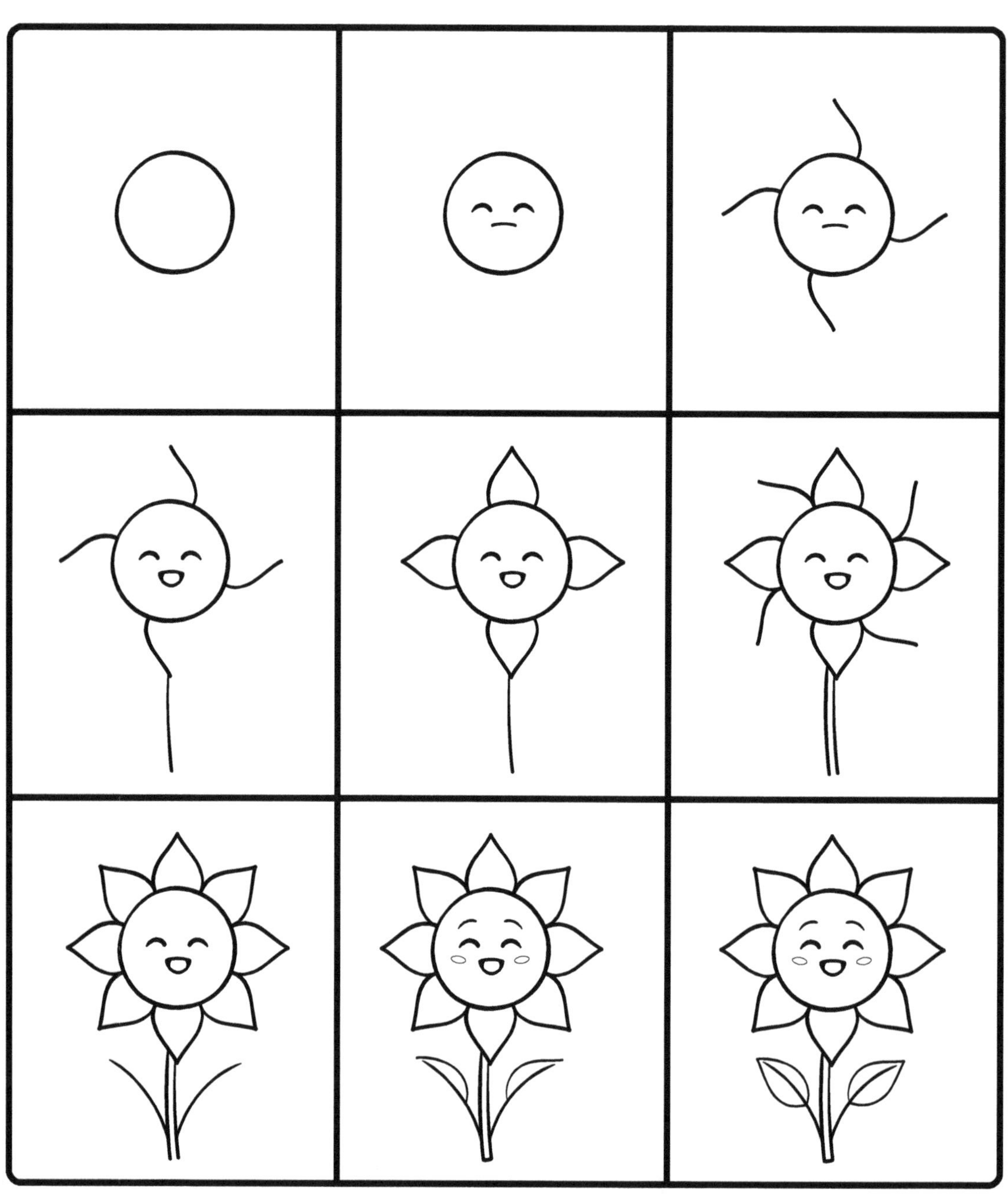

CRUMBIE

LIVES:

IN A CUPBOARD WAITING TO BE EATEN.

LOVES:

THE BREEZE ON MY FROSTING WHEN THEY BLOW MY CANDLES AND MAKE A WISH.

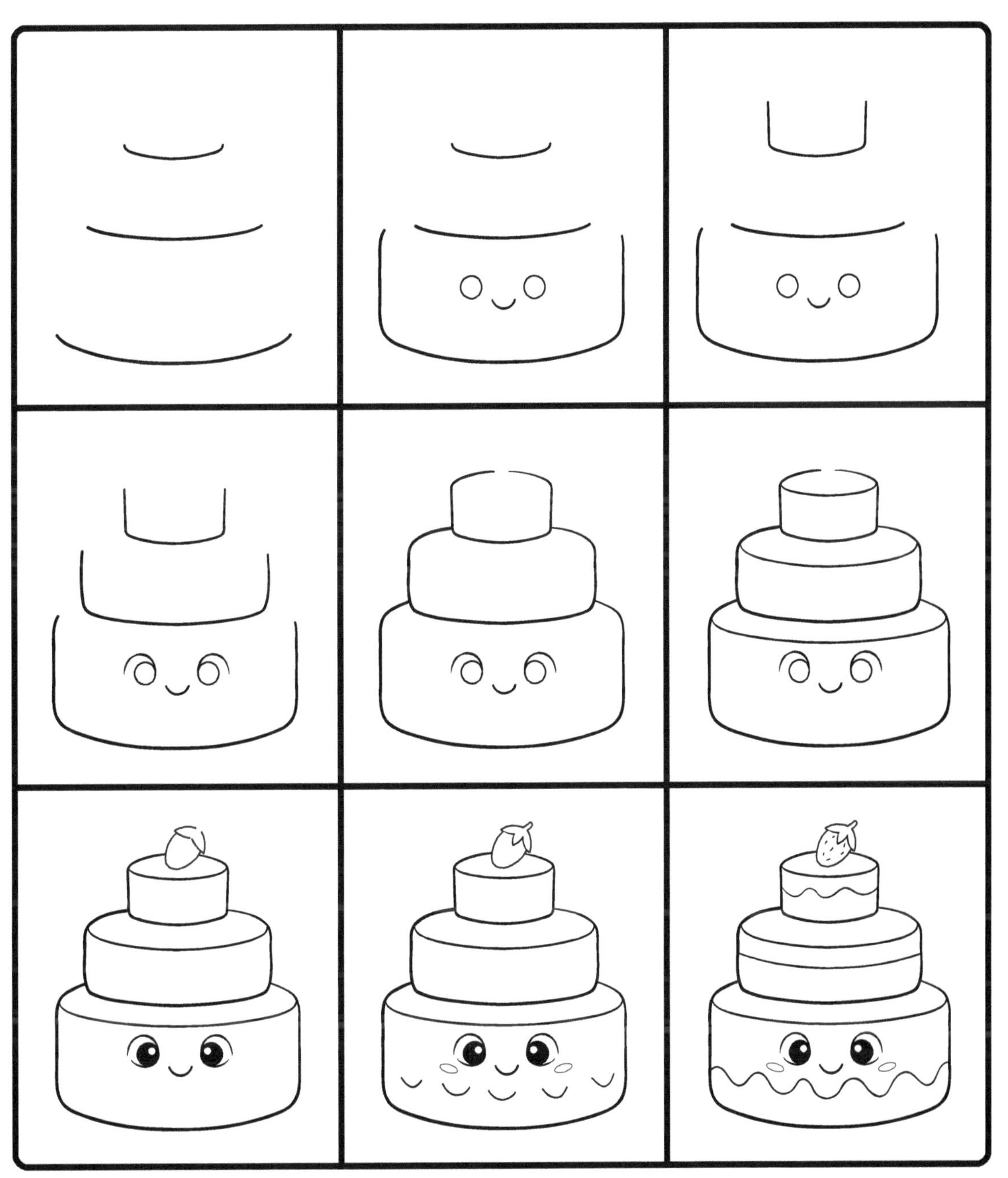

CHUTIE-CUTIE

LIVES:

IN A BAKERY.

LOVES:

GOING TO BIRTHDAYS AND BEING THE STAR OF THE PARTY!

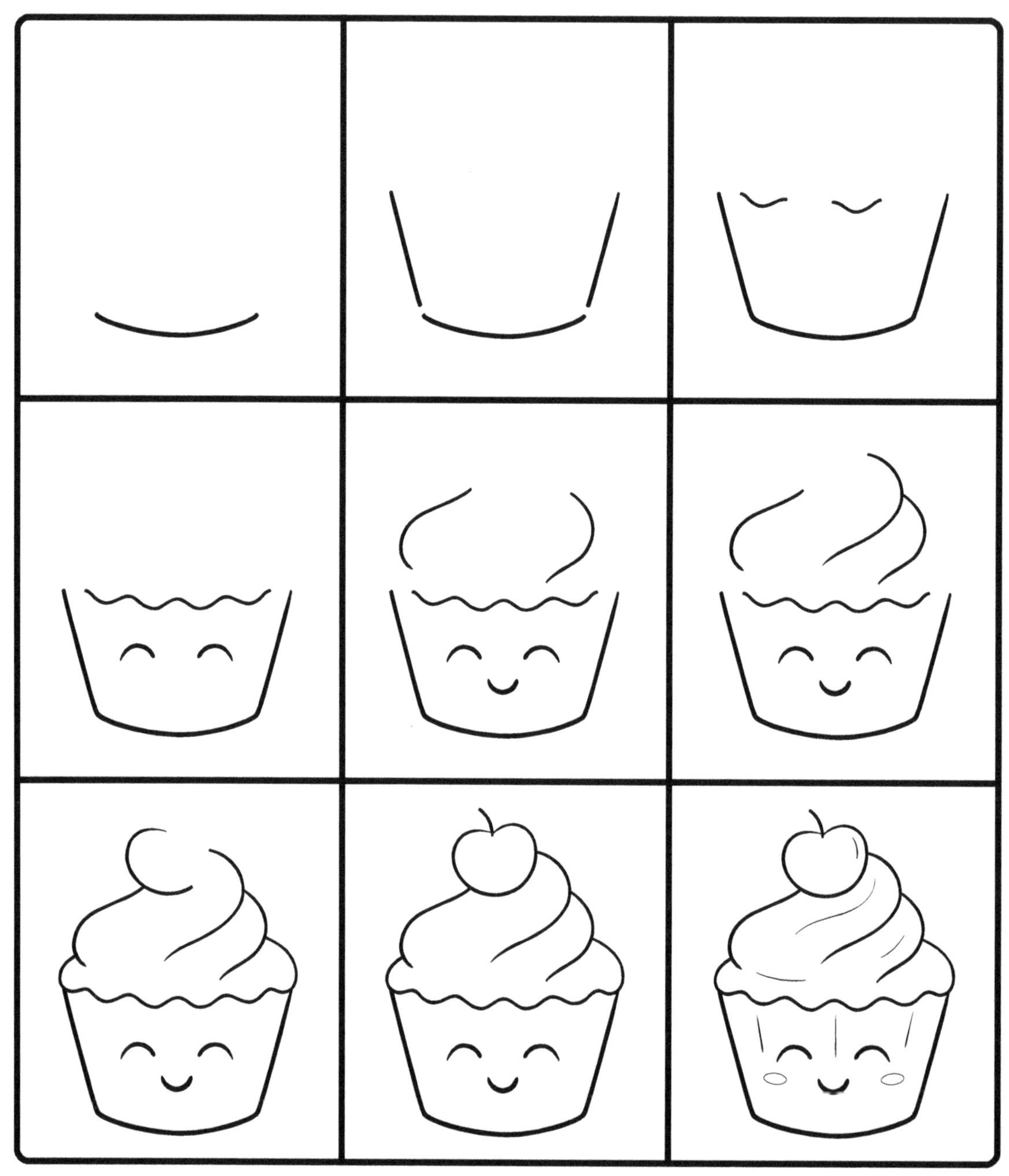

DUDE

LIVES:

IN A BASKET IN A TIKI HUT BY THE BEACH.

LOVES:

BEING TURNED INTO A SUMMER DRINK, AND HOW THE STRAW TICKLES HIS BELLY!

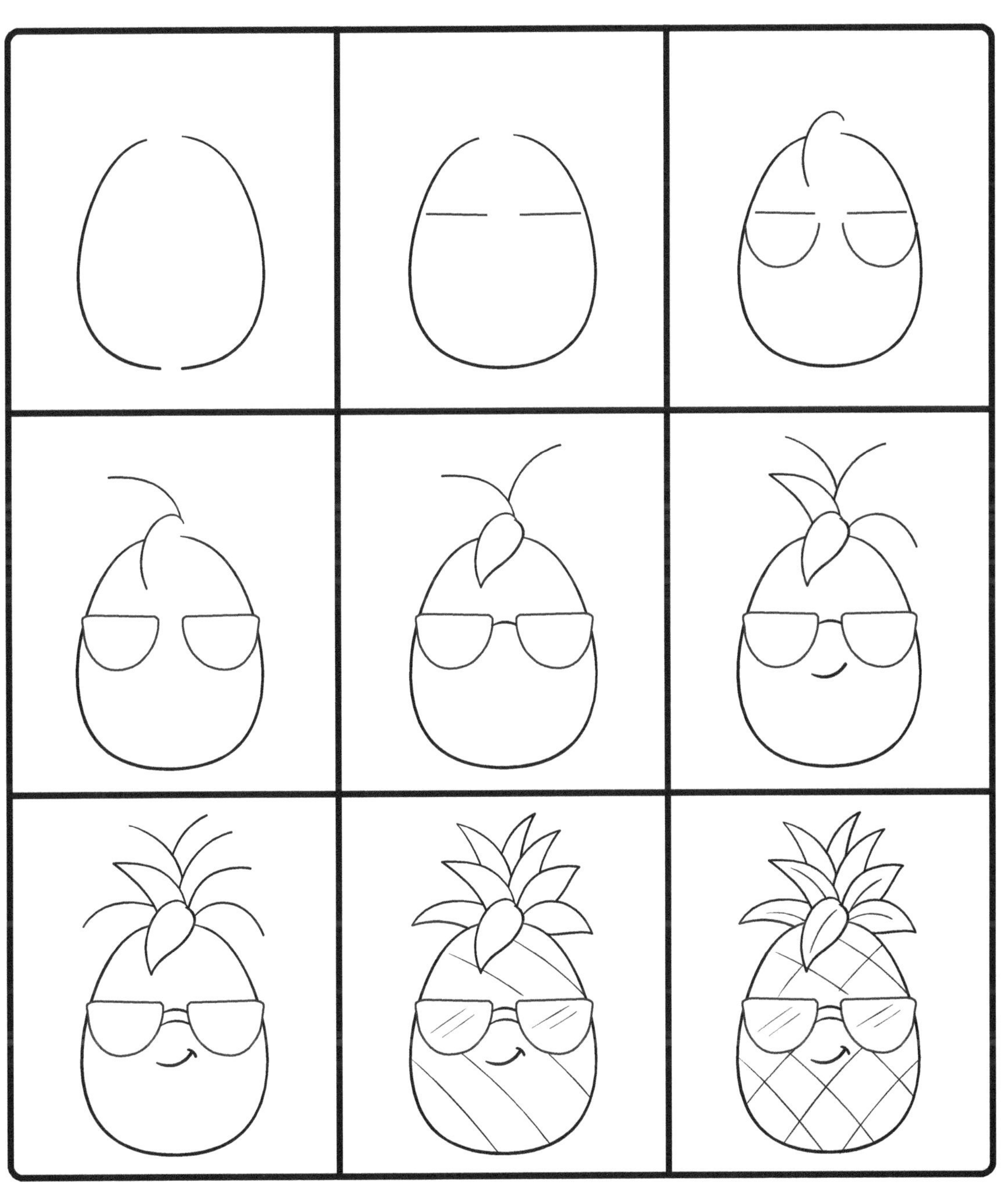

GREEN TIP

LIVES:

IN A SUNNY FIELD, SURROUNDED BY SUNFLOWERS AND BUTTERFLIES.

LOVES:

BEING MADE INTO A HALLOWEEN LANTERN AND LIGHTING UP THE PORCH.

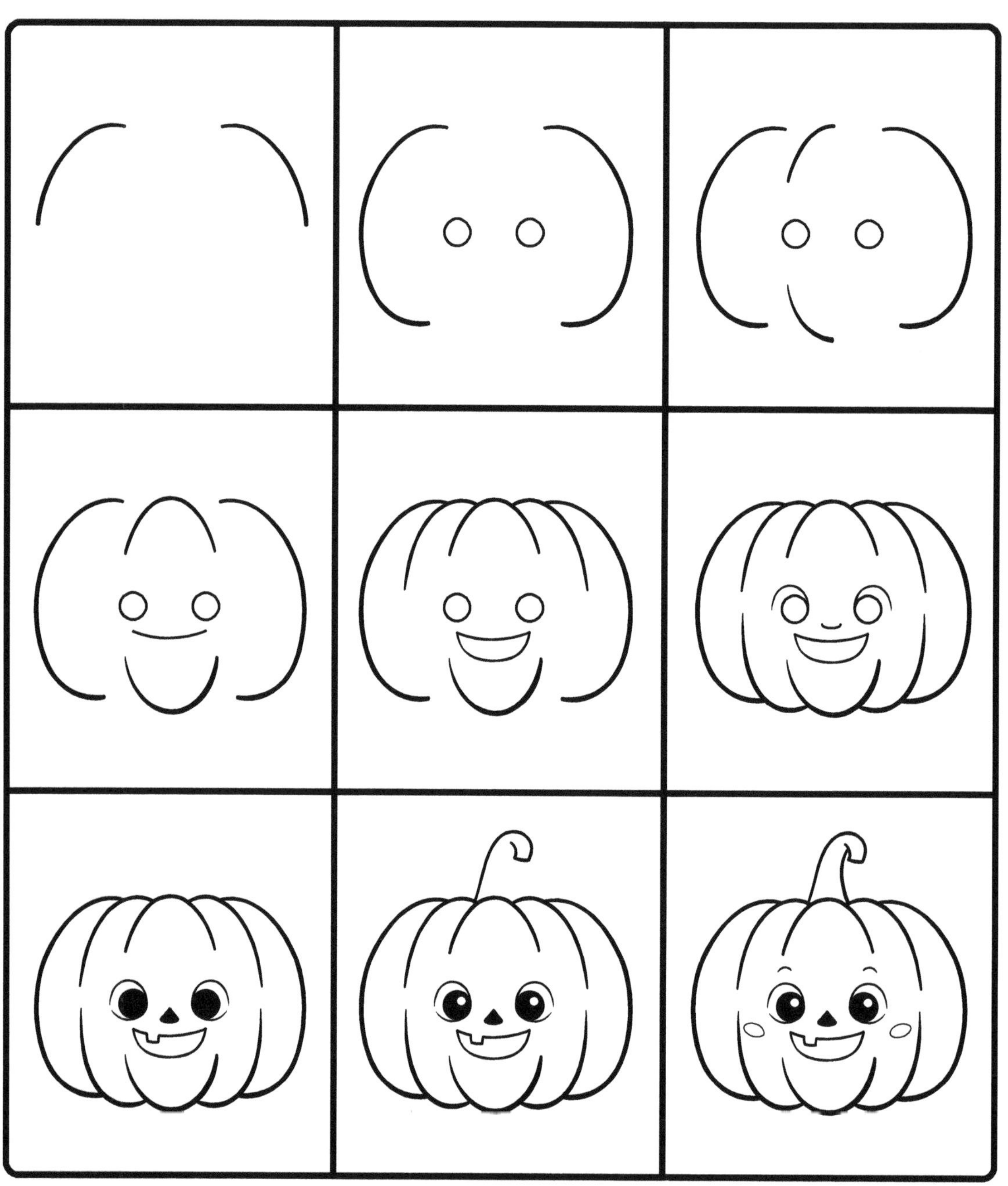

SLURP

LIVES:

IN A BOX IN THE GARAGE.

LOVES:

BEING PUT IN A LUNCHBOX AND TAKEN TO SCHOOL – THERE IS SO MUCH TO LEARN!

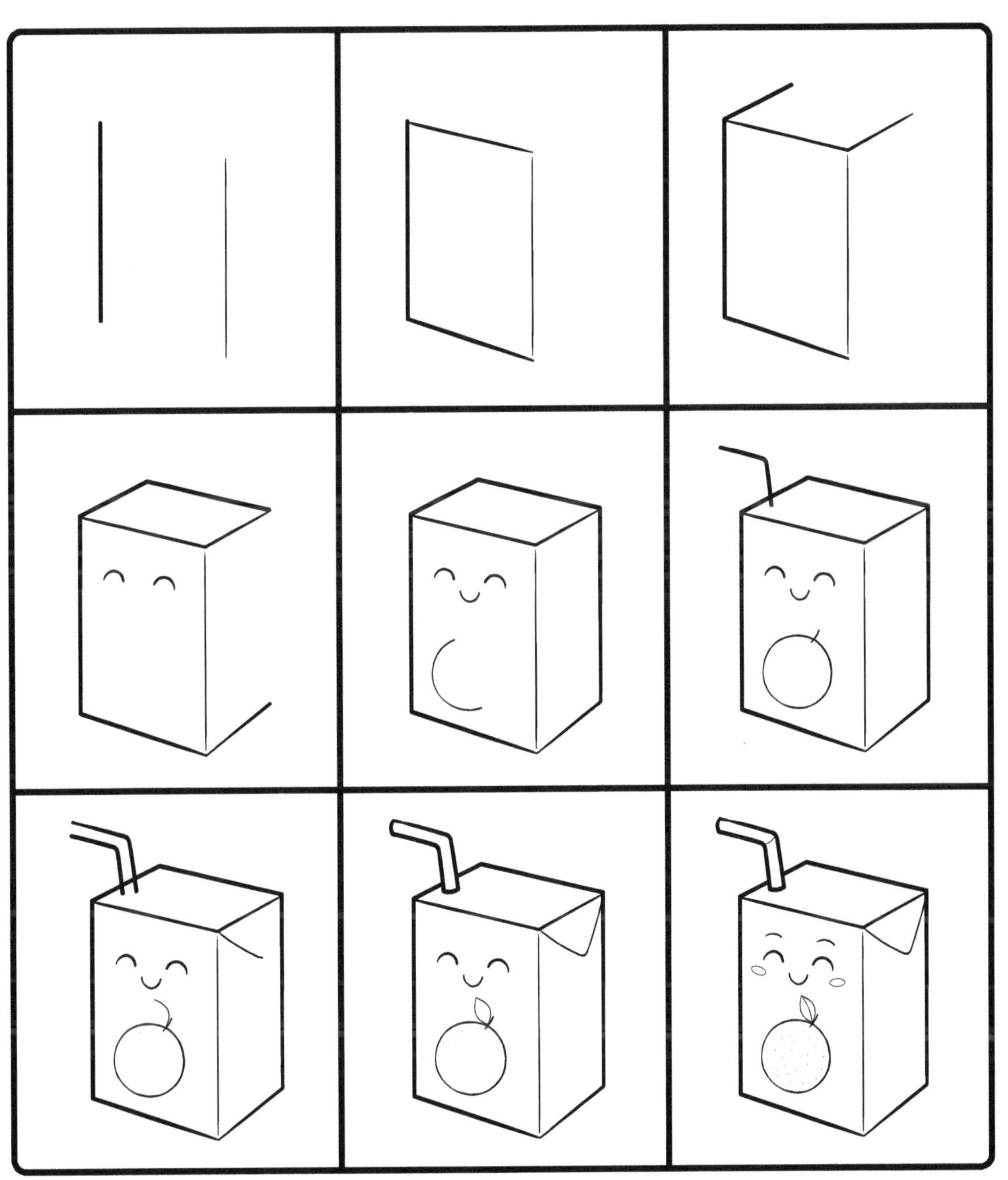

DASH

LIVES:

UPSTAIRS FROM THE RESTAURANT HE WORKS IN.

LOVES:

COOKING, IT'S SO EASY WITH AN INSTANT FLAME!

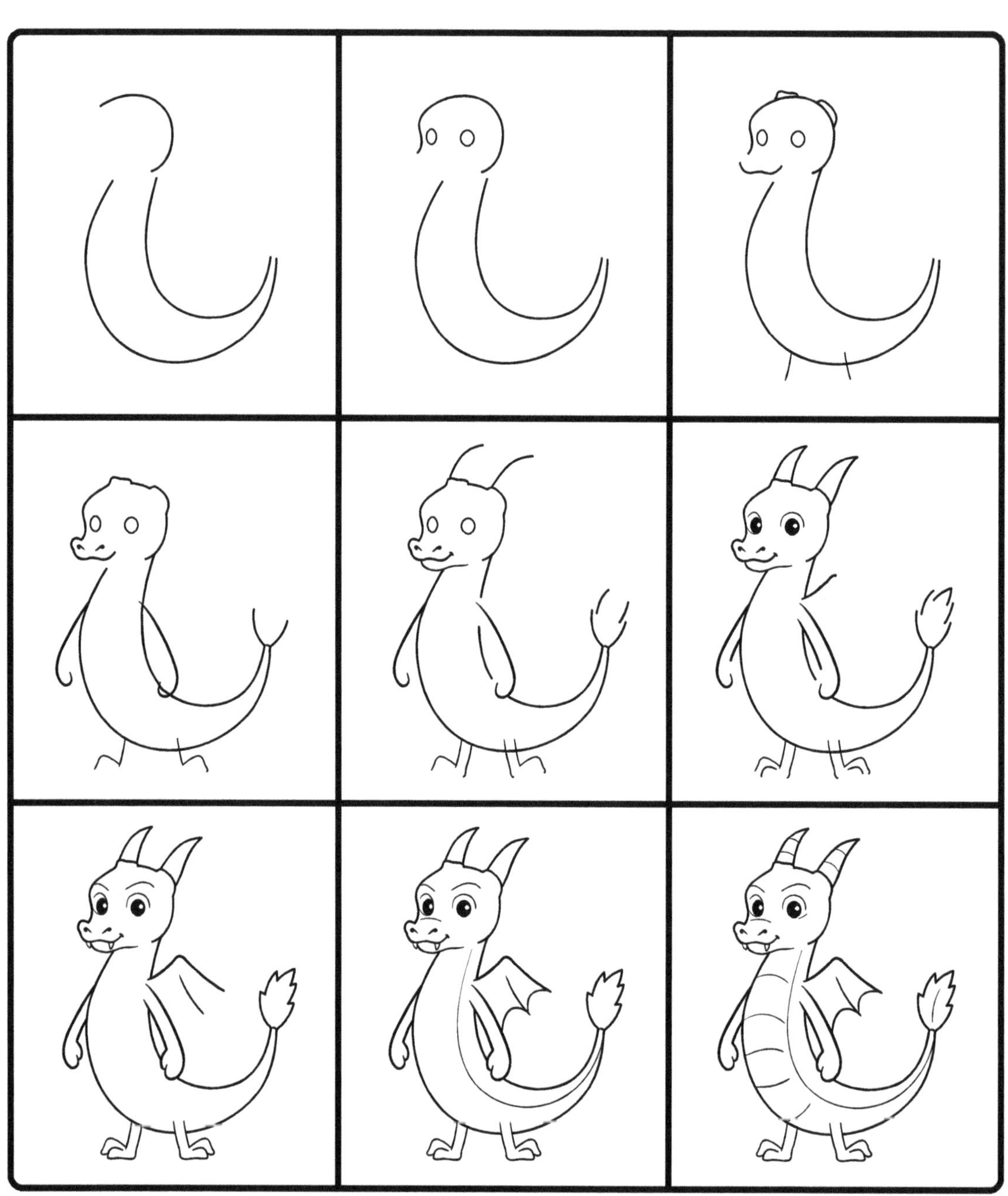

SPLASH

LIVES:

IN THE ATLANTIC OCEAN.

LOVES:

BEING BIG AND BEAUTIFUL, BUT IT WOULD BE REALLY COOL TO BE ABLE TO CAMOUFLAGE LIKE SEAHORSES DO.

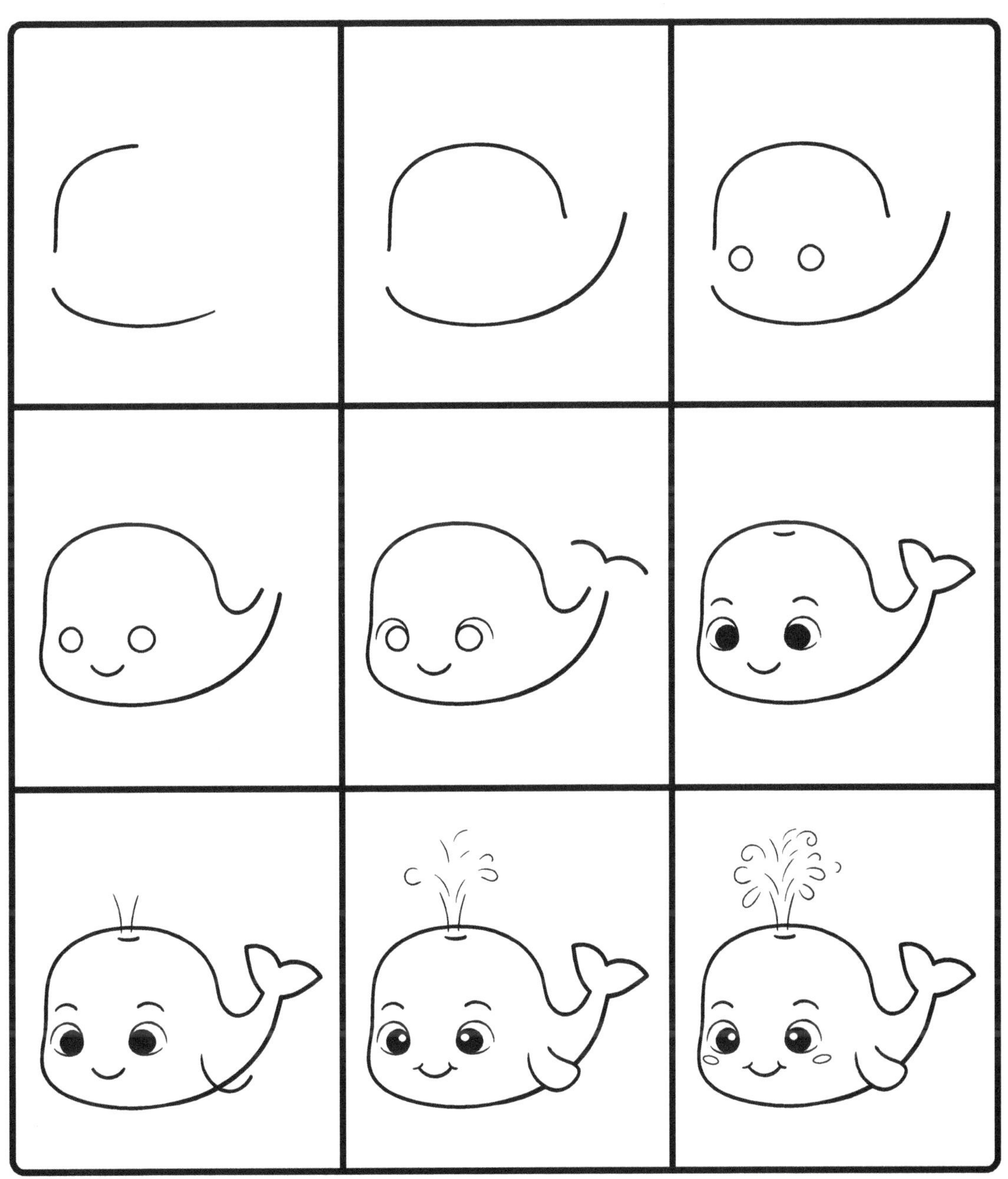

SWISSY

LIVES:

ON A FARM, SURROUNDED BY GREEN GRASS, COWS, AND A SHEEPDOG.

LOVES:

THE SWISS ALPS, THE BEST PLACE IN THE WORLD!

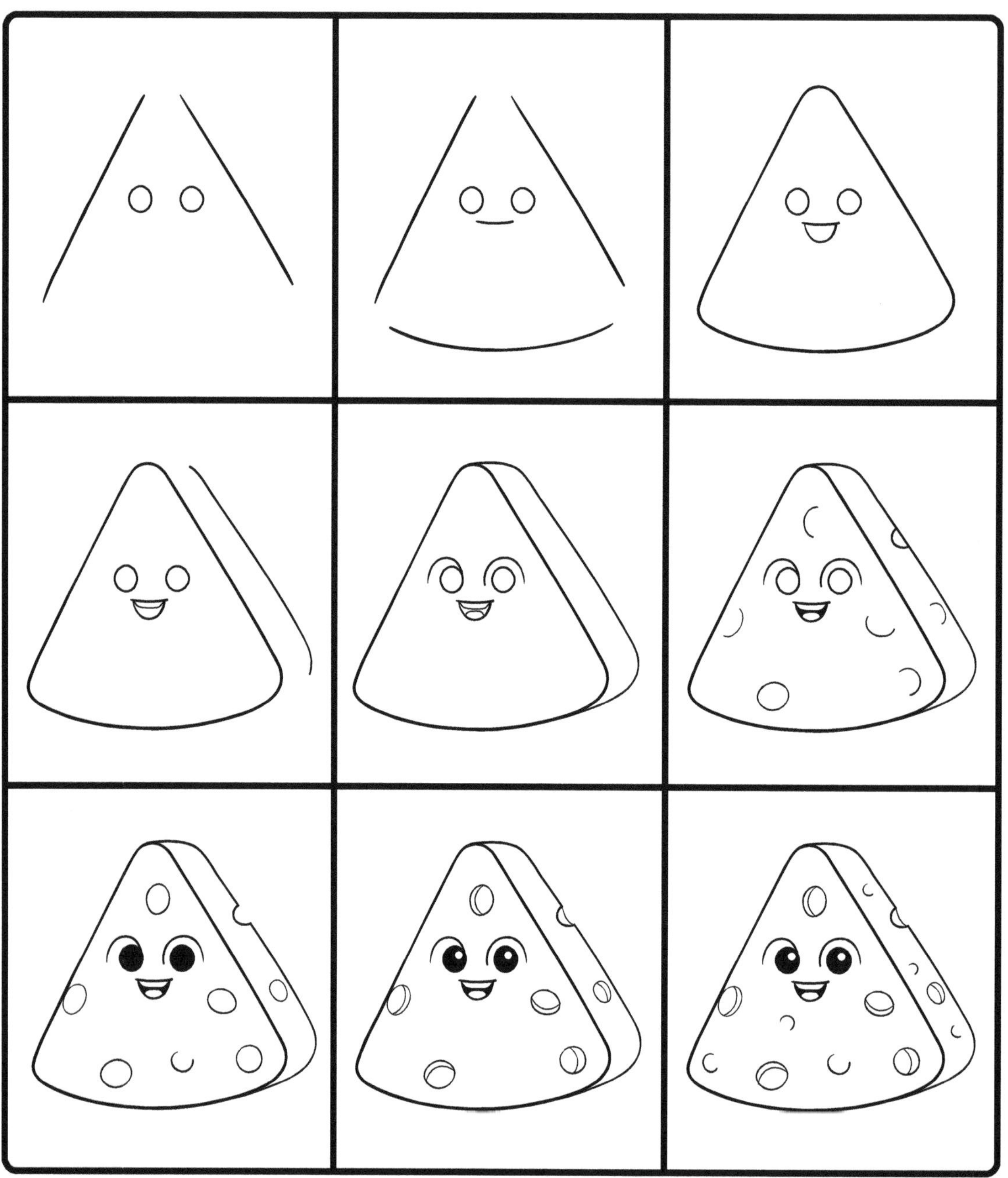

LEGGY

LIVES:

ON THE ROAD WITH HIS TRAVELING BAND.

LOVES:

BEING ABLE TO PLAY SO MANY INSTRUMENTS AT ONCE!

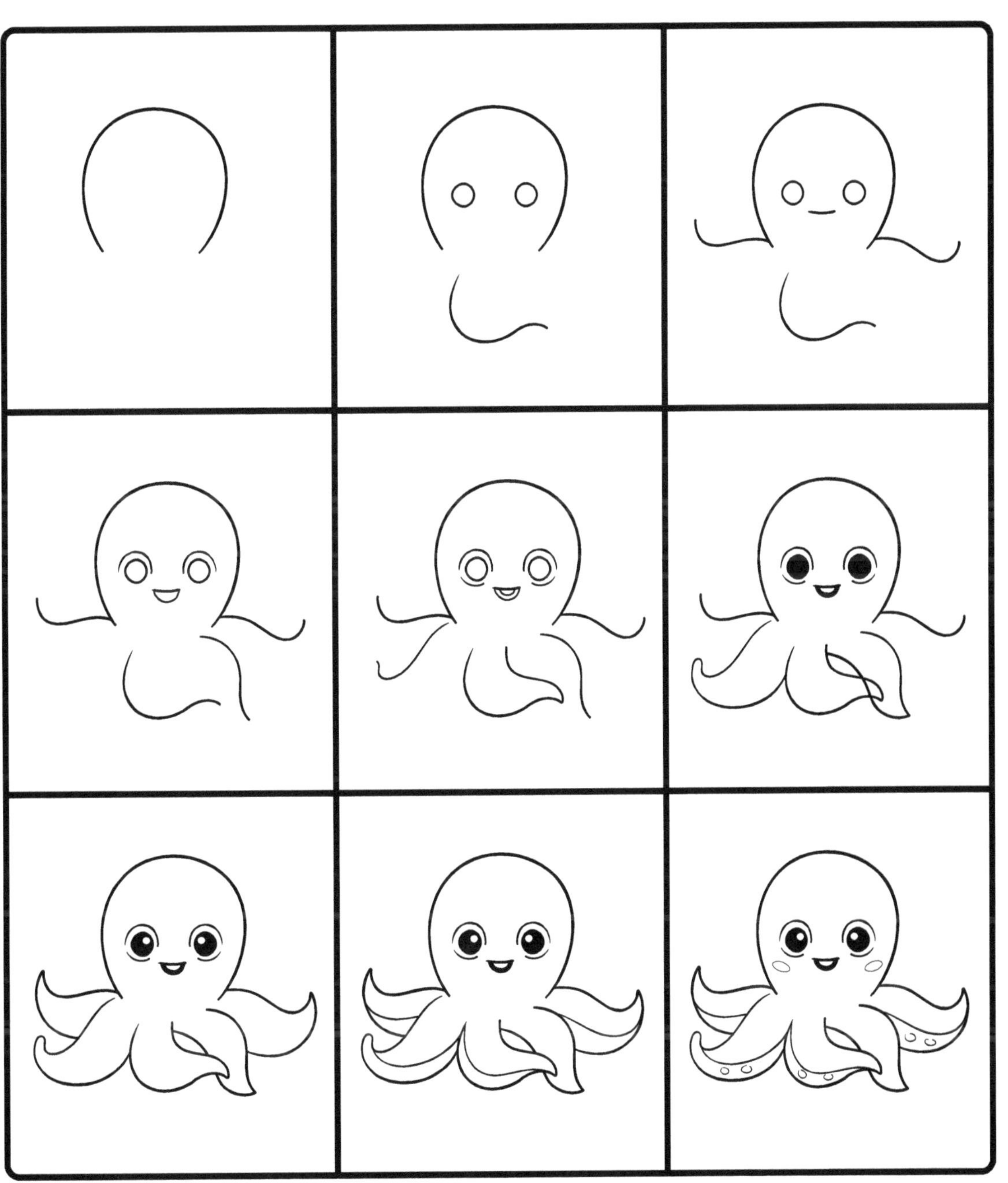

PUNG

LIVES:

IN THE NORTH POLE.

LOVES:

ICESKATING WITH HER FRIENDS.

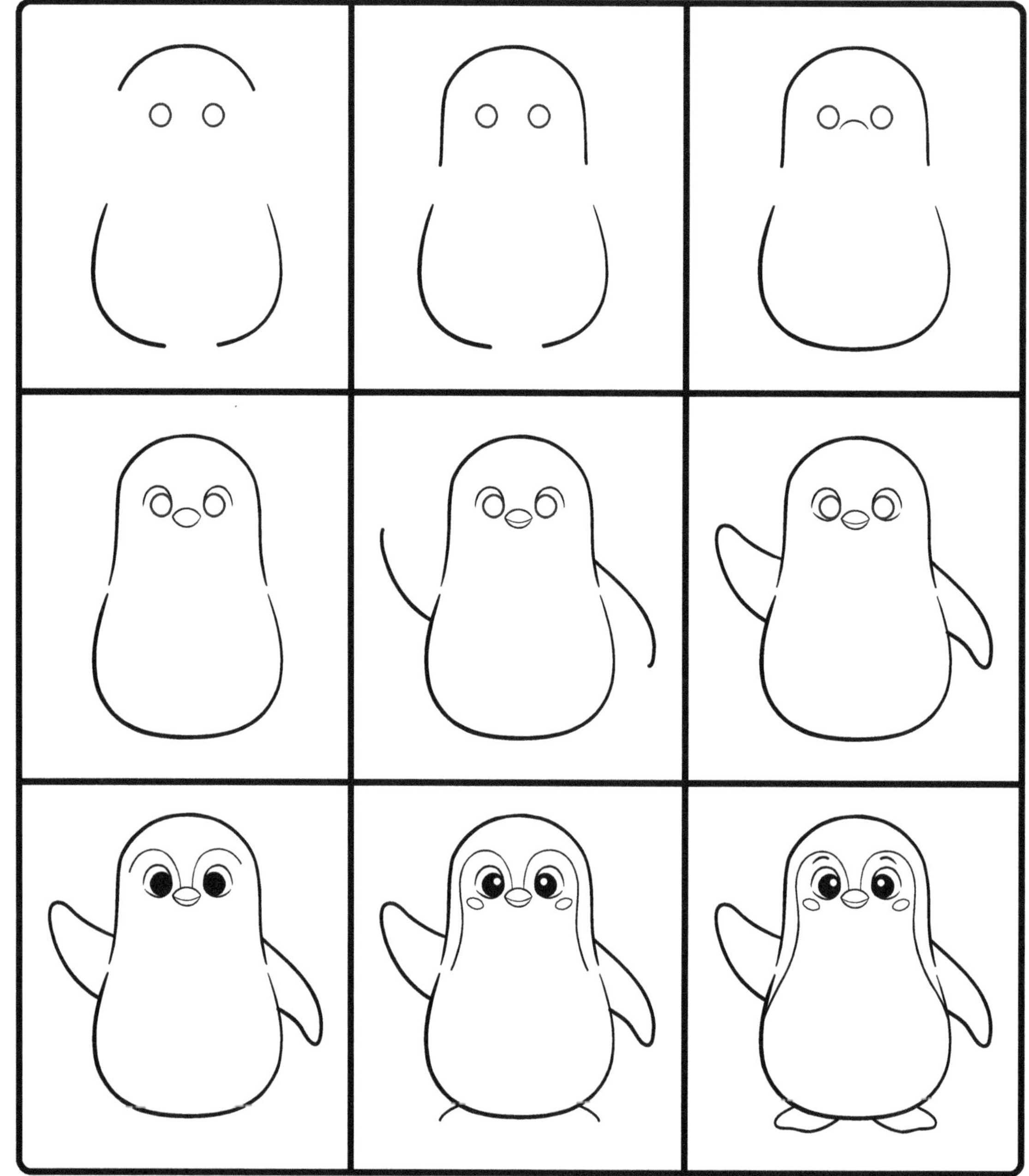

BOXY

LIVES:

IN A GIFT SHOP.

LOVES:

WAITING UNDER THE TREE ON CHRISTMAS MORNING.

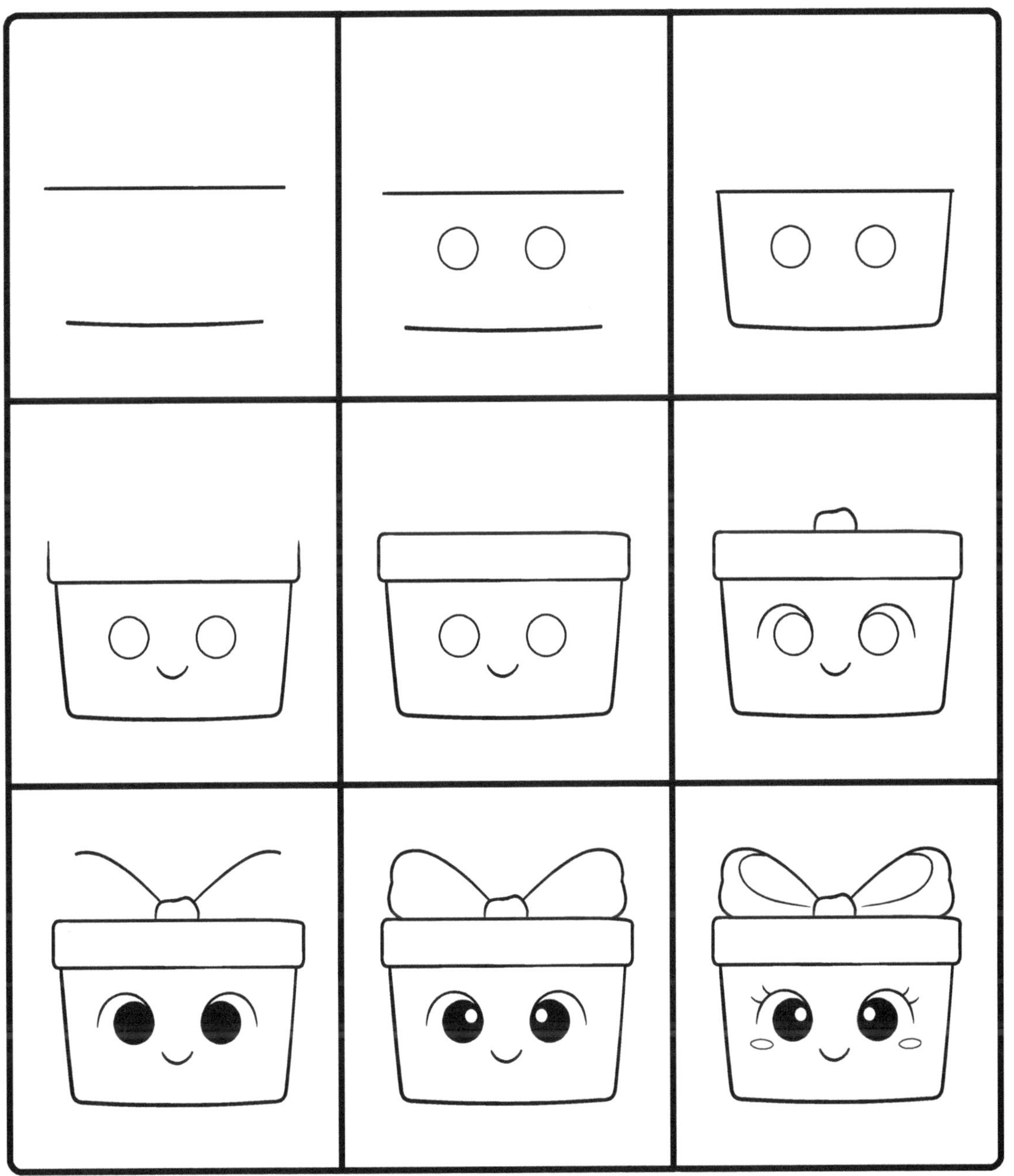

SPROUT

LIVES:

AT A NURSERY.

LOVES:

THE SAFETY OF LIVING IN A POT, BUT WOULD SO LOVE TO STRETCH ITS ROOTS OUT ONE DAY.

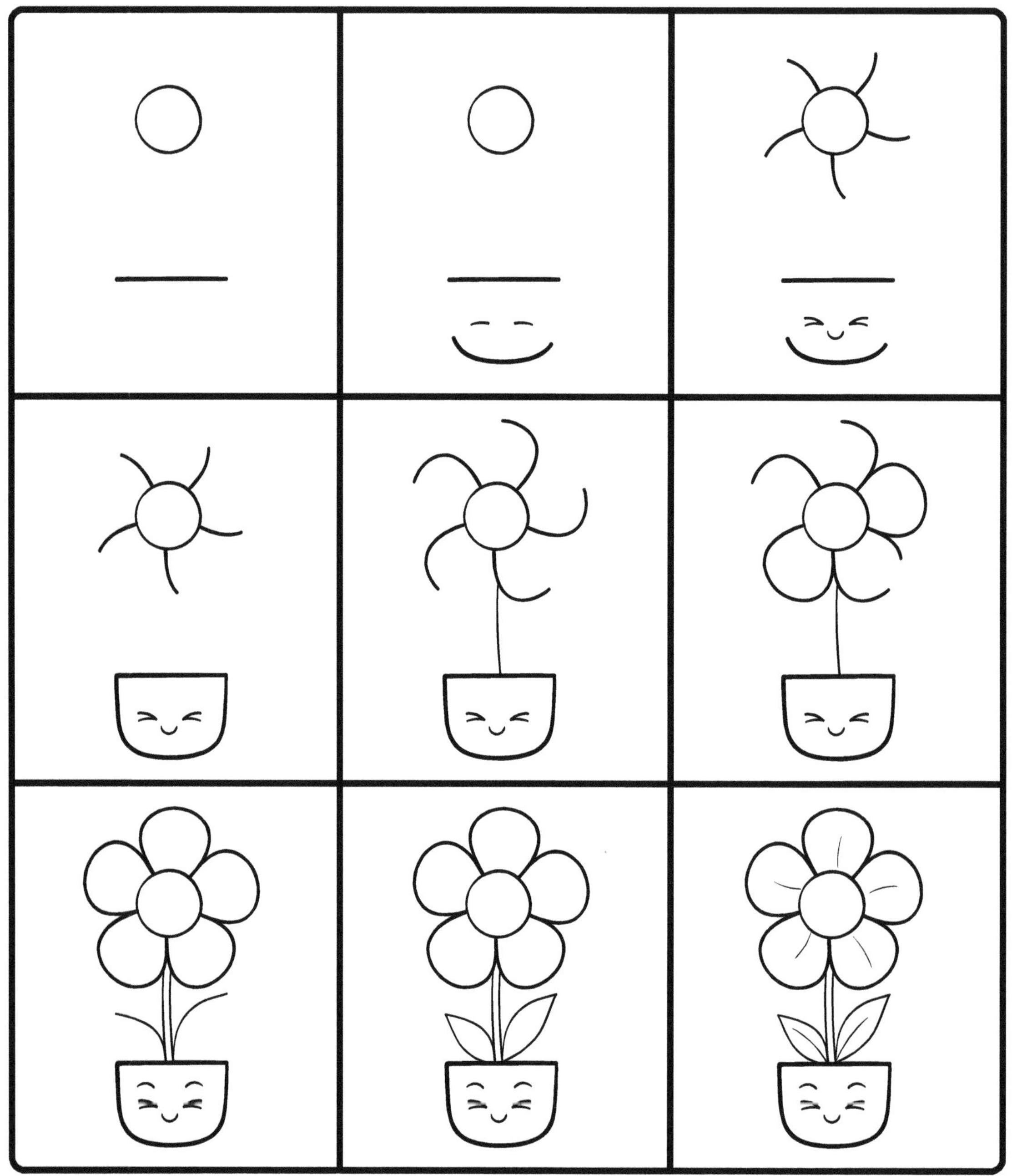

CHEEPER

LIVES:

IN A CHOOK PEN IN A YARD.

LOVES:

BEING LITTLE AND HELD IN SMALL WARM HANDS.

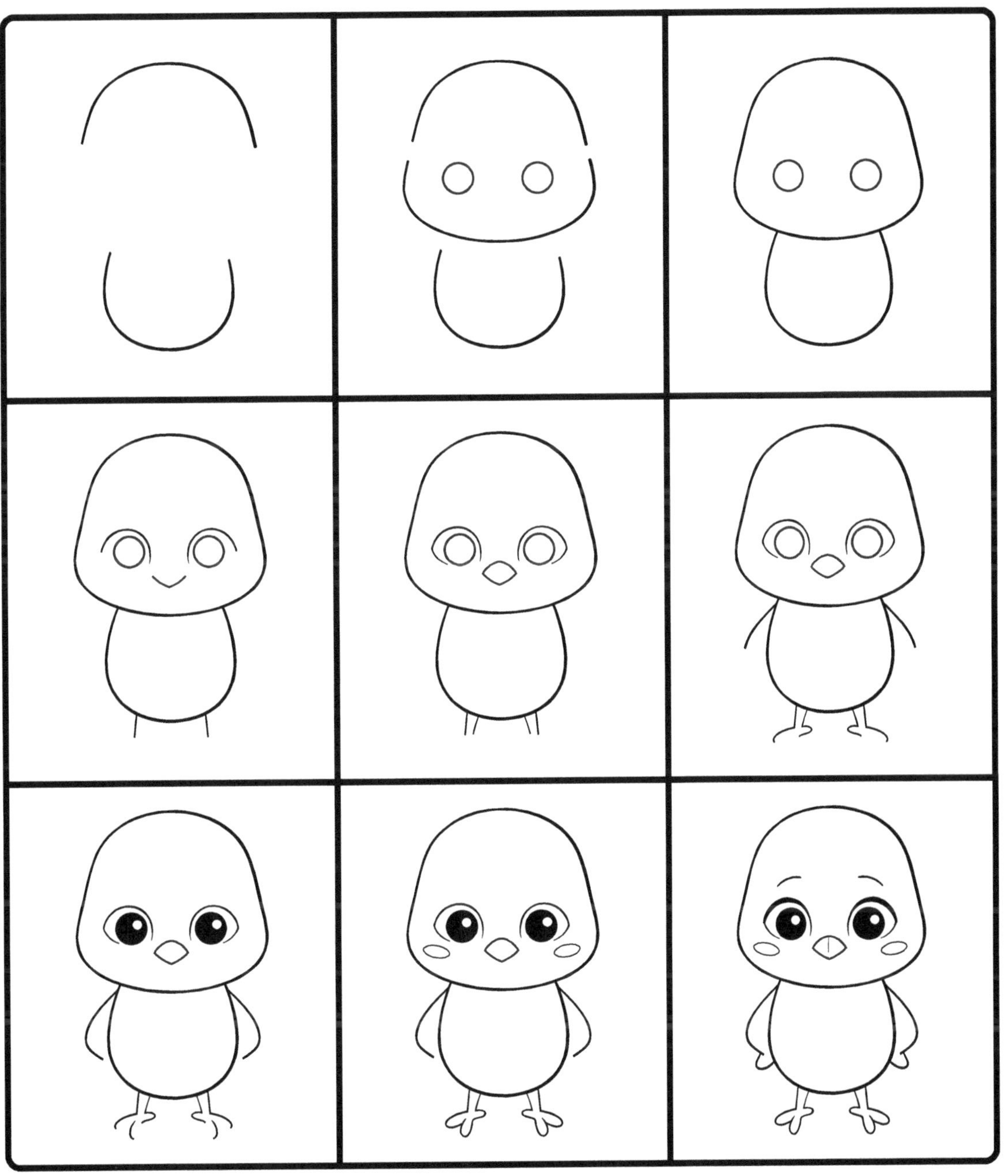

CHUM

LIVES:

IN A REMOTE FOREST.

LOVES:

THE IDEA OF BEING IN THE CHIPMUNK BAND IN THE BIG CITY.

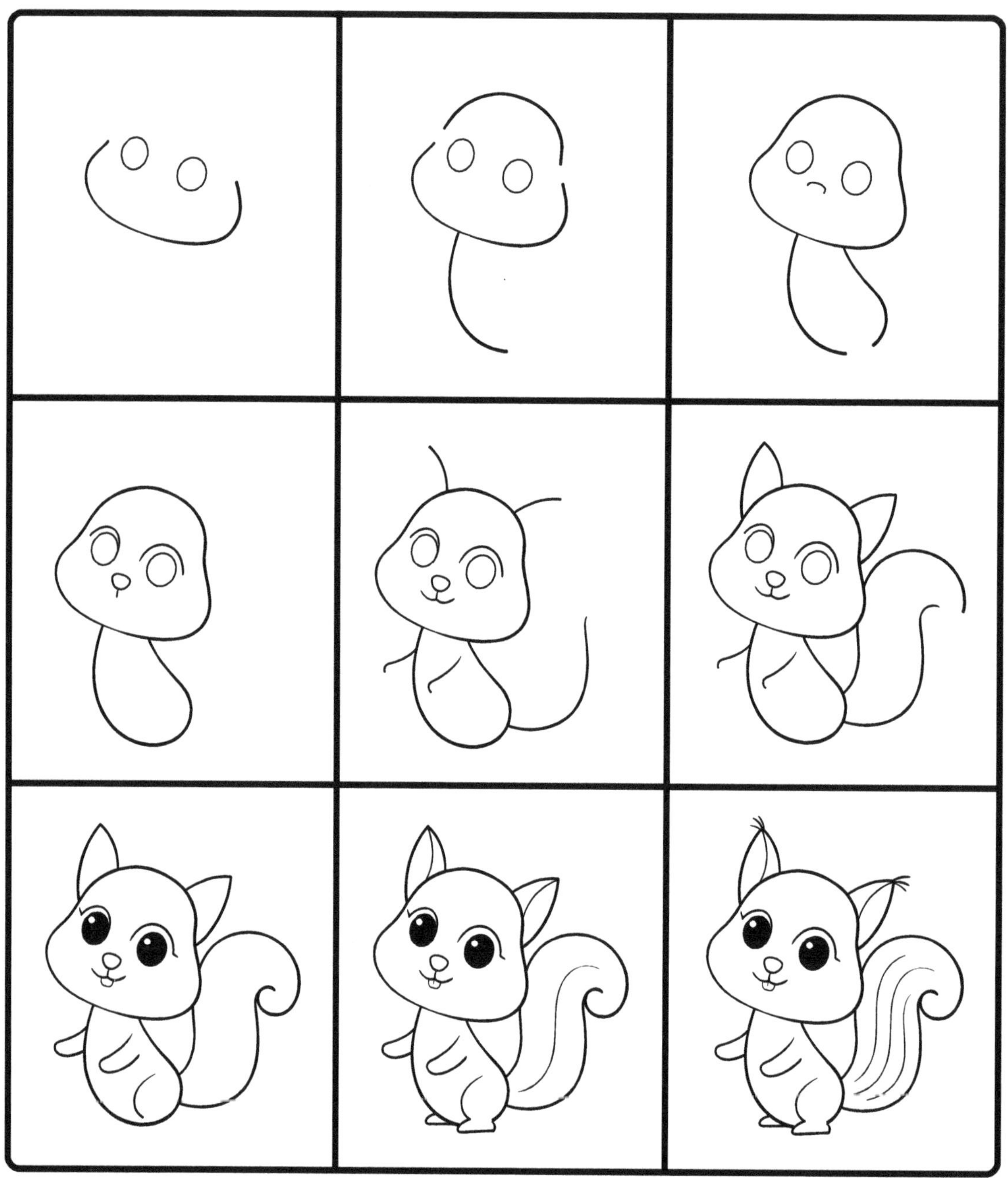

SWIRL

LIVES:

ON A SUPERMARKET SHELF.

LOVES:

ROLLING OVER SUGAR AND CINNAMON, SO SWEET!

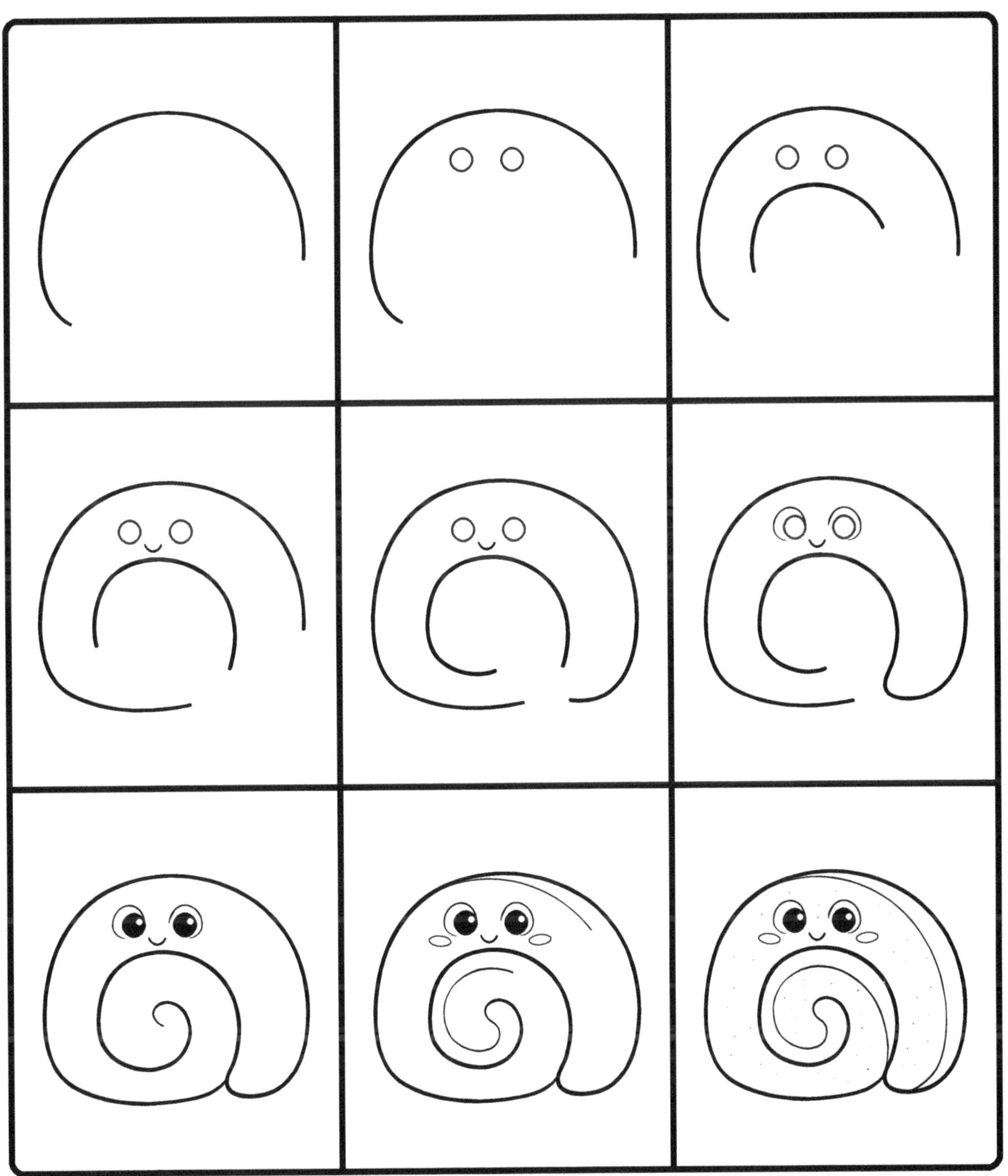

NOO-NOO

LIVES:

IN A RAMEN SHOP IN DOWNTOWN TOKYO.

LOVES:

BEING SLURPED! AND CAN'T UNDERSTAND WHY IN SOME COUNTRIES IT'S RUDE TO SLURP!

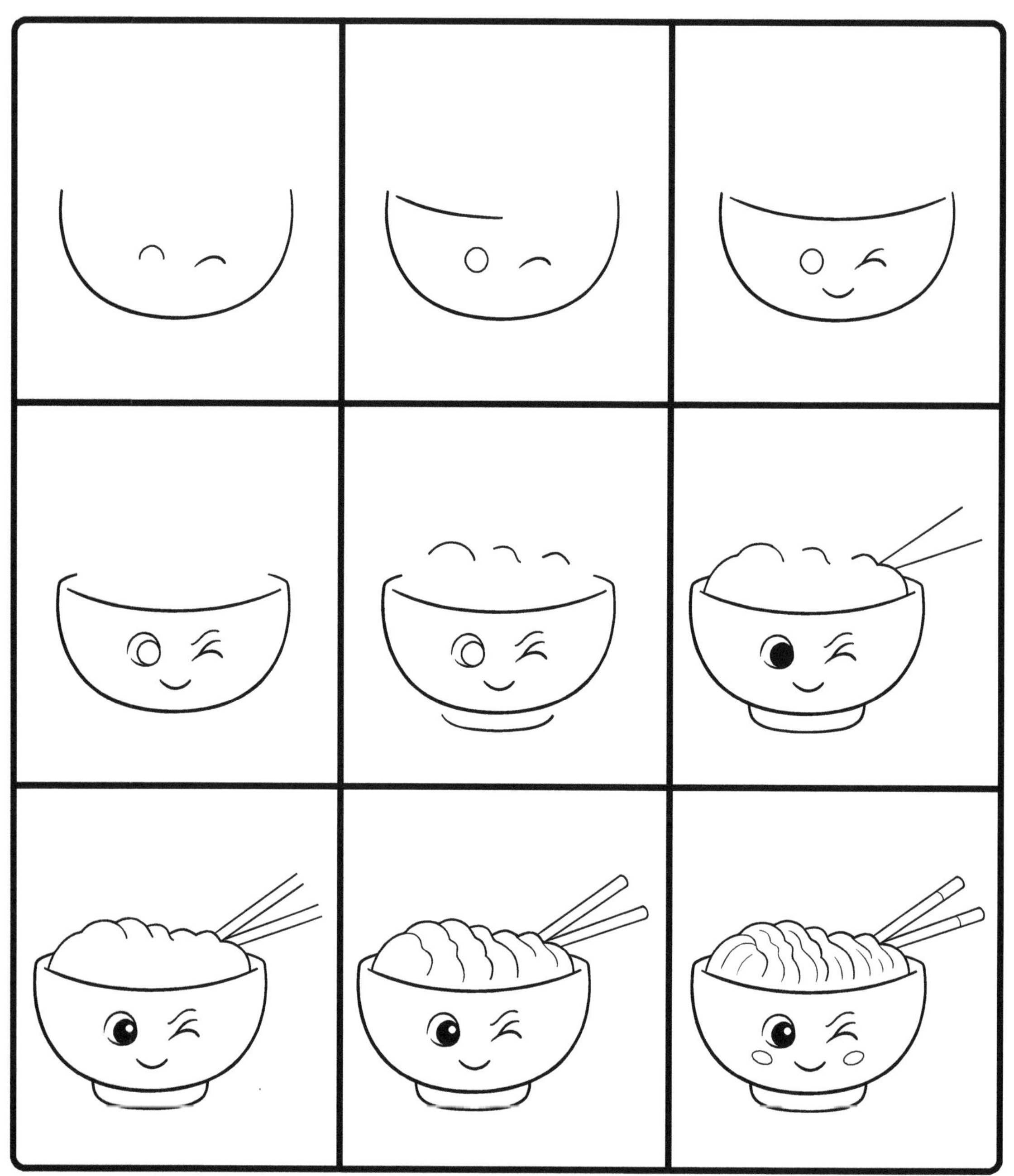

CONCLUSION

SO HOW DID YOU GO DRAWING THE CHIBI CHARACTERS? WERE SOME TRICKIER THAN OTHERS? OR SOME MORE FUN TO DRAW?

NOW THAT YOU KNOW THE BASICS OF DRAWING EACH CHIBI, YOU CAN ADD YOUR OWN UNIQUE TOUCHES AND PERSONALITIES TO THEM!

IF YOU ENJOYED THE BOOK, PLEASE BE SURE TO LEAVE US A REVIEW ON AMAZON AS IT REALLY HELPS US GROW!

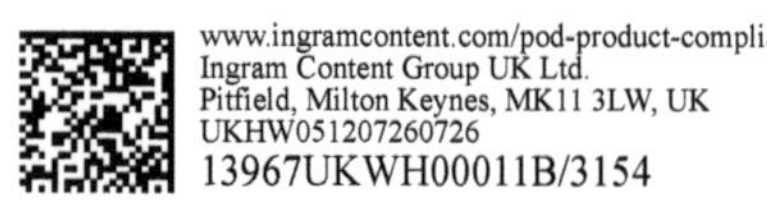

www.ingramcontent.com/pod-product-compliance
Ingram Content Group UK Ltd.
Pitfield, Milton Keynes, MK11 3LW, UK
UKHW051207260726
13967UKWH00011B/3154

9 781922 805171